THE SHAPE OF UTOPIA

The Shape of Utopia
Studies in a Literary Genre

Robert C. Elliott

THE UNIVERSITY OF CHICAGO PRESS
Chicago and London

PN
56
U 8E5

Standard Book Number: 226–20500–2
Library of Congress Catalog Card Number: 78–103136
The University of Chicago Press, Chicago 60637
The University of Chicago Press, Ltd., London

In memory of my friend
Sigurd Burckhardt

Contents

Preface

Just as in utopia it is easier to specify what has been avoided than what has been achieved, so it is easier to say what this book is not than what it is. It is not a history of utopias. Although the essays herein take into account most of the best-known literary utopias, including negative ones, and some fairly obscure examples of the kind, there is no attempt whatever at historical coverage. Ideology is not the central concern here either, although any study of a genre so imbedded in social and political issues must have its own ideological biases. I have not tried to conceal my own deep ambivalence about utopian modes of thought.

The essays that follow are of two kinds: interpretive studies of individual literary utopias and genre studies of the utopian mode itself. They are connected by certain thematic interests that run through the book. One of the themes is structural and, I suppose, functional; it has to do with the relation of utopian literature to satire: the use of utopia as a strategy of satire, the distribution of positive and negative elements in the two genres. Gonzalo's utopian speech in *The Tempest* reflects the theme in part:

> *I' the commonwealth I would by contraries*
> *Execute all things; for no kind of traffic*
> *Would I admit; no name of magistrate;*
> *Letters should not be known; riches, poverty,*
> *And use of service, none. . . .*
> *All things in common nature should produce*
> *Without sweat or endeavour; treason, felony,*
> *Sword, pike, knife, gun, or need of any engine,*

> *Would I not have; but nature should bring forth*
> *Of its own kind, all foison, all abundance,*
> *To feed my innocent people.*

If this has more of a Golden Age than a utopian flavor about it, still Gonzalo expresses the characteristic negative emphasis of the literature which issues from man's fantasies about what life on earth could be like.

A second theme, which is moral and political, may be summed up in the Latin phrase *corruptio optimi pessima:* the corruption of the best becomes the worst; or, as Shakespeare puts the same sentiment,

> *sweetest things turn sourest by their deeds;*
> *Lilies that fester smell far worse than weeds.*

The theme has shadowed utopia from the beginning. It has particular significance for our day because of its importance in feeding the flood of negative utopias that in the last forty or fifty years has swept away most of our dreams of a better world.

Generous and large-spirited as many of those dreams were, some were foolish and some dangerous. Although the uninhibited utopianizing imagination which produced them is alive again in certain areas of our culture (among the hippies, for example), as a motivating force for major social change it has for good reason nearly disappeared. Our history has made confident visions of the wholesale reconstitution of society, like those of the nineteenth century, impossible. Significantly, the New Left refuses to spell out details of the society it hopes to establish. On the other hand, without an image of the good life to guide him man loses his will to invent and shape the future: as Mannheim says, he becomes a thing. Our writers, no longer able to construct blueprints of the desirable life of the future, may find that necessity adds glamour to more modest goals. Kenneth Boulding welcomes the historical period on which we have entered—post-civilization, he calls it—because it offers the possibility that slavery, poverty, exploitation, gross inequality, war, and disease—"these prime costs of civilization"—will fall to the vanishing point. We still have the chance to make the transition to this "modest utopia," says Boulding—a chance which is probably not repeatable in this part of the universe. Late as it is, there is still meat here for the literary imagination.

A word on terminology: *utopia* is notoriously a tricky term as, given its birth in ambiguity, it must be. The word has broad and restricted meanings, positive and pejorative ones. Except that I write Utopia with a capital to indicate a place, I can make no claim to consistency of usage, relying instead on context to make clear the sense intended for the term and its derivatives at any given point.

The first, second, and fifth essays of this book appeared, in different form, in *Yale Review*, *ELH*, and *Centennial Review*, respectively. The first and the fifth essays appeared in German translation in *Antaios*. The sixth essay appeared in Italian translation in the issue of *Strumenti Critici* devoted to American criticism (June 1969). The fourth essay was written originally for *Hawthorne Centenary Essays*. Editors of these publications have kindly given me permission to use the essays here. The third essay was presented in different form as a paper at the Second International Congress on the Enlightenment, held at St. Andrews University, Scotland, in August 1967.

I am glad to be able to thank publicly the people and the institutions who have helped me in the preparation of this book. In critical and creative ways my graduate students made me learn as I tried to teach. I have worked in the Widener Library at Harvard, the British Museum, the Bibliothèque Nationale in Paris, and the libraries at

Ohio State University and the University of California, San Diego. My work has been supported by the Guggenheim Foundation and the American Council of Learned Societies. These are utopian institutions every one, and I am most grateful for their indispensable aid. Although it would not be entirely accurate to speak of either Ohio State University or the University of California as utopian, I am equally grateful for the research grants and the support of various kinds they generously provided. Jan Altizer has been a most able editorial assistant. Several of my friends have read part or all of this work at one stage or another of its development: Morton W. Bloomfield, Leicester Bradner, Sigurd Burckhardt, Robert M. Estrich, Richard Falk, Sydney Harth, Kurt H. Wolff, Andrew Wright, and particularly Roy Harvey Pearce. I thank them all for their criticisms and suggestions—for their interest. Much more than thanks to Mary, who does not believe in utopia.

THE SHAPE OF UTOPIA

1

Saturnalia Satire & Utopia

Engels once spoke of Charles Fourier, the nineteenth century's complete utopian, as one of the greatest satirists of all time. The conjunction may seem odd; we normally think of utopia as associated with the ideal, satire with the actual, which (man and his institutions being what they are) usually proves to be the sordid, the foolish, the vicious. In fact, however, the two modes—utopia and satire—are linked in a complex network of genetic, historical, and formal relationships. Some of these I propose to trace.

First, a tangle of genetic lines which, in the way of these matters, lead to unexpected places. "All Utopias," writes Arthur Koestler, "are fed from the sources of mythology; the social engineer's blueprints are merely revised editions of the ancient text." Insofar as utopia incorporates man's longings for the good life, it is part of a complex of ideas that includes the Golden Age, the Earthly Paradise, the Fortunate Isles, the Islands of the Blest, the Happy Otherworld, and so on. The archetypal text, at least for the Western world, is that of Hesiod:

> *In the beginning, the immortals*
> *Who have their homes on Olympos*
> *created the golden generation of mortal people.*
> *These lived in Kronos' time, when he*
> *was the king in heaven.*
> *They lived as if they were gods,*
> *their hearts free from all sorrow,*
> *by themselves, and without hard work or pain;*
> *no miserable*
> *old age came their way; their hands, their feet,*
> *did not alter.*
> *They took their pleasure in festivals,*
> *and lived without troubles.*
> *When they died, it was as if they fell asleep.*
> *All goods*
> *were theirs. The fruitful grainland*
> *yielded its harvest to them*
> *of its own accord; this was great and abundant,*
> *while they at their pleasure*
> *quietly looked after their works,*
> *in the midst of good things*
> *prosperous in flocks, on friendly terms*
> *with the blessed immortals.* [1]

For the fifth race of man, for us of the iron age, it was a good dream and it lasted, as Lionel Trilling has indicated,

1. *The Works and Days*, in *Hesiod*, trans. Richmond Lattimore (Ann Arbor: University of Michigan Press, 1959), pp. 31–33.

until it was dispossessed by the nightmare of Dostoevski's Underground Man.

Variations of Hesiod's story probably existed long before his time in folktales of a magical land of plenty where wine runs in rivers and pancakes grow on trees. At any rate the Greek comic writers picked up these themes as a handy way of satirizing the literature of the Golden Age, which even then (as ever since) was sadly stereotyped. An early example of the satire is this from Teleclides:

> First there was peace among all things like water covering one's hands. And the earth bore neither fear nor disease, but all needed things appeared of their own accord. For every stream flowed with wine, and barley cakes fought with wheat cakes to enter the mouths of men. . . . And fishes, coming to men's houses and baking themselves, would serve themselves upon the tables. . . . and roasted thrushes with milk cakes flew down one's gullet.[2]

The references to peace and to freedom from fear and disease make the target of the parody clear enough; but parody or no, there is inevitable doubleness of effect— longing as well as laughter. Tales of Cockaigne turn up in the folklore of many lands, nearly always with similar effects. An English version from the early fourteenth century makes Cockaigne out to be fairer than Paradise. Here is an abbey built entirely of food, where geese fly roasted from the spit advertising their own succulence: "Geese, all hot, all hot!" Here are rivers of oil and milk and honey and wine along which lusty monks chase willing nuns. Here (with the negative emphasis necessary in these matters) is no strife, no pain, no death. These

2. See Arthur O. Lovejoy and George Boas, *Primitivism and Related Ideas in Antiquity* (Baltimore, Md.: Johns Hopkins Press, 1935), pp. 40–41.

lines (in a modern version by A. L. Morton) emphasize the longing:

> *In Cockaigne we drink and eat*
> *Freely without care and sweat. . . .*
> *Under heaven no land like this*
> *Of such joy and endless bliss.*

> *There is many a sweet sight,*
> *All is day, there is no night,*
> *There is no quarreling nor strife,*
> *There is no death but endless life. . . .*

> *Every man takes what he will,*
> *As of right, to eat his fill.*
> *All is common to young and old,*
> *To stout and strong, to meek and bold.*[3]

On the other hand, much of the poem is satirical; but satire is easily overwhelmed in such express outpouring of desire. One finds the same longing and the same laughter in "The Big Rock Candy Mountain," a song sung in the United States by men on the bum in the 1930s. Cockaigne knows no limitations of space or time: in its untrussed moments every age shares Sir Epicure Mammon's dream of "a perpetuitie / Of life, and lust." America's Rock Candy Mountain is an authentic part of Cockaigne's lush landscape.

The Golden Age and Cockaigne provide the elements out of which the intellectual concept of utopia develops. We can see this happening in the literature of ancient Greece; Plato's adoption of the gold, silver, brass, and iron imagery from Hesiod to make palatable the "noble

3. *The English Utopia* (London: Lawrence and Wishart, 1952), pp. 217–22.

lie" of *The Republic* is an emblem of the process. When belief in the historical reality of the Golden Age broke down, it became possible to bring many of the ideal elements of the myth into closer relation with the realities of man's existence. Philosophers transferred the notion of an ideal life in the irrecoverable past into utopian tales of what the world might—even should—be like; the myth, that is, provided sustenance for a conceivable reality. It has been the same ever since.

The Golden Age and utopia, the one a myth, the other a concept, are both projections of man's wishful fantasies, answering to the longings for the good life which have moved him since before history began. "Véritable rêve de paysan fatigué": so Maurice Croiset characterizes Hesiod's account of the Golden Age. Utopia comes ultimately from the same dream. Identity of origin, however, by no means implies identity of function. Plato, undertaking the Socratic search for the meaning of justice, is led to conceive an ideal social order—a utopia; but justice, the object of his search, would be USELESS, as David Hume emphatically put it, in a society like that of the Golden Age.[4] The contours and customs of these ideal lands are very different indeed. In Utopia, the work of the world goes on, rationalized, cleaned up—often to the point where sewers hardly smell—given dignity; the work is there, nevertheless, as a necessary condition of Utopia's existence. In Cockaigne, says the song, "they hung the jerk that invented work." Sebastian de Grazia makes the distinction thus: "Utopia is a possessor of culture; Cockaigne is possessed by the folk."[5]

4. "Of Justice," *The Philosophical Works*, ed. T. H. Green and T. H. Grose (Darmstadt: Scientia Verlag Aalen, 1964), 4:179 ff.

5. *Of Time, Work, and Leisure* (New York: Twentieth Century Fund, 1962), pp. 377–82.

A dialogue of Lucian neatly points up the functional difference. Just before the annual celebration of the feast of the Saturnalia, Cronosolon complains to the tutelary god Cronus about his poverty. Look, he says, how many pestilent rich fellows there are these days, while I and others like me, skilled in the liberal arts, have only want and trouble for bedfellows. And you, Cronus, will not "order things anew, and make us equal." [6]

"In common life," answers Cronus, "'tis no light matter to change the lots that Clotho and her sister Fates have laid upon you; but as touching the feast, I will set right your poverty." The point is this: for the period of the Saturnalia, Cronosolon and his fellows will enjoy the good things of life on the same footing as the rich. During this sacred time the Golden Age will come again to earth— that, after all, is the meaning of the festival. But this is a very different matter, Cronus points out, from changing the way things are in common life and making everybody equal; such affairs are in his son Zeus's jurisdiction, not in his. Clearly, if one does not believe in Zeus's good will, or even in his existence, these become matters for man alone. Utopia is the application of man's reason and his will to the myth. For the Golden Age is given by the gods, like the millennium in Christian eschatology, independently of man's will. To be sure, heretical religious sects, intoxicated with dreams of millennial bliss, have tried to establish paradise on earth by fiat; some of the bizarre results are brilliantly documented in Norman Cohn's *Pursuit of the Millennium*. But Utopia is different: Utopia (in the sense we are concerned with here) is man's effort to work out imaginatively what happens—or what might happen—when the primal longings embodied in

6. "Cronosolon," in *Works*, trans. H. W. Fowler and F. G. Fowler (Oxford: Clarendon Press, 1905), 4:113 ff.; cf. "Saturnalian Letters," 4:120 ff.

the myth confront the principle of reality. In this effort man no longer merely dreams of a divine state in some remote time; he assumes the role of creator himself.

A characteristic of the Golden Age, whatever the version, is that it exists outside history, usually before history begins: *in illo tempore*. In Hesiod's account, it is true, men are timebound in the sense that they finally die—*Et in Arcadia ego*—but only after long lives joyously lived, without the sufferings of old age. Other variations of the paradise myth speak of a timeless, changeless, deathless existence, as in Hesiod's own description of the Islands of the Blest, where the heroes who fought at Troy and Thebes live in perpetual joy; or as in the Irish myth of the voyage of Bran which in a stroke or two superbly dramatizes the distinction between mythical time and the time of history. Bran and his men sail back to Ireland after having spent indeterminate ages in the Happy Otherworld. As they approach land, Bran calls out to a man on shore: "I am Bran, the son of Febal." The man responds: "We do not know such a one, though the Voyage of Bran is in our ancient stories." Then one of Bran's men leaps from the coracle to shore. "As soon as he touched the earth of Ireland, forthwith he was a heap of ashes, as though he had been in the earth for many hundred years." [7] Paradise is necessarily transhistoric.

Planners of Utopia have often tried to approximate that condition, aiming at a static perfection which would rule out the vicissitudes of history and to some degree those of time. Sparta, Athens, and Rome would not now be lying in ruins, wrote Jerome Busleyden in the sixteenth century, if they had known and followed the laws expounded in Thomas More's great *Utopia*: "On the contrary,

---

7. *The Voyage of Bran*, trans. Kuno Meyer (London: David Nutt, 1895), p. 32.

they would have been still unfallen, still fortunate and prosperous, leading a happy existence, mistresses of the world meanwhile."[8] As with states, so with men: it is a rare utopia that does not broach the theme of immortality or greatly increased longevity in one form or another, from elixirs in Bacon's *New Atlantis* to application of evolutionary theory in twentieth-century utopias. The attempt of utopian writers to freeze history—the fight of utopia against history—has prompted severe criticism of the whole utopian enterprise; but the attempt has been merely one way in which man has tried to arrive imaginatively at the condition of paradise on earth.

Ritual has provided another approach to the same state. The annual feast commemorating the reign of Cronus (in his Roman form, Saturn) was avowedly a reenactment of the Golden Age—a return to the time when all men were equal and the good things of life were held in common. Out of his primal authority Cronus reserved a few days in the year, he says in one of Lucian's dialogues, so that "men may remember what life was like in my days."[9] The happy anarchy of his rule was recollected in Roman law which held that during the Saturnalian festival war could not be begun nor could criminals be punished—for what was war and who were criminals in the Golden Age? Lucian's dialogues convey marvelously the atmosphere of the Saturnalia, but at the same time they are permeated by his characteristic skepticism. Most celebrants are likely to have had a different attitude, to have felt that, for the few days of celebration, they were reliving the myth, actually participating in the far-off age at the beginning of things which answered to their deepest longings. The Saturnalia

8. In Thomas More, *Utopia*, ed. J. H. Lupton (Oxford: Clarendon Press, 1895), p. 315.
9. "Saturnalia," *Works*, 4:111.

were more than an excuse to get drunk and (like Horace's slave in the famous Satire) to say aloud what one thought of one's superiors; they were themselves an abrogation of time. In all imitations of archetypes, writes Mircea Eliade, "man is projected into the mythical epoch in which the archetypes were first revealed." Profane time and history are abolished in the act of celebration, for one "is always *contemporary with a myth*, during the time when one repeats it or imitates the gestures of the mythic personages."[10] Thus the divine efficacies of the Saturnalia made present the joy that had been irrevocably lost from earth. Through the alchemy of ritual the age of iron was temporarily transmuted into gold.

The forms that the Saturnalia take allow us to see what the memory of a Golden Age really means. To reenact it is to experience the extravagant joy of overthrowing the restraints, the inhibitions and renunciations, which, as the price we pay for civilization, trammel us relentlessly in the real world. The theme of the Saturnalia is reversal—reversal of values, of social roles, of social norms. The real world is a world peopled normally by a few camels and many ants, in Lucian's image; under the dispensation of ritual it becomes a place where discrepancies disappear and all become equal. The Saturnalia are ruled over, not by a camel, but by a king chosen by lot; slaves sit down with their masters and are served by them; everyone speaks as he wills, eats and drinks as he pleases (as though Nature again produced lavishly for all), and enjoys a sexual liberty unthinkable at any other time. The Saturnalia mean release.

In some of the cognate festivals of Western Europe the release is spectacularly explosive. Consider the

10. *The Myth of the Eternal Return*, trans. W. R. Trask (London: Routledge & Kegan Paul, 1955), p. 35; *Myths, Dreams and Mysteries*, trans. Philip Mairet (London: Harvill Press, 1960), p. 30.

Feast of Fools as it was celebrated in Paris at New Year's in the fifteenth century. This is from a contemporary account:

> Priests and clerks may be seen wearing masks and monstrous visages at the hours of office. They dance in the choir dressed as women, panders, or minstrels. They sing wanton songs. They eat black puddings at the horn of the altar while the celebrant is saying mass. They play at dice there. They cense with stinking smoke from the soles of old shoes. They run and leap through the church, without a blush at their own shame. Finally they drive about the town and its theatres in shabby traps and carts; and rouse the laughter of their fellows and the bystanders in infamous performances, with indecent gestures and verses scurrilous and unchaste.[11]

Again, reversal and release. The words of the Magnificat —"He hath put down the mighty from their seats, and exalted them of low degree"—triggered the revelry of the Feast of Fools. It was an affair largely of the lower clergy (E. K. Chambers calls it an "ebullition of the natural lout beneath the cassock") who, like the lower orders at the Saturnalia, could on this occasion turn distinctions of rank and status upside down, subject the ceremonial forms which ordered their lives to wild burlesque, give way to verbal and sexual license in a great outburst of pent-up repression. All order is repressive, not least that of the Church. The Feast of Fools is an anarchic blow at order, like the pagan feast at Rome a reaching out for a state of "pure" freedom.

In these rites which temporarily turn society inside out, ridicule, mockery, burlesque—in short, satire, using the word in its broad sense—seem always to have important functions. A characteristic of saturnalian festivals everywhere is that during the license of the holiday the most

11. Translated by E. K. Chambers in *The Medieval Stage* (London: Oxford University Press, 1903), 1:294.

sacred institutions may be subjected to mockery and sacrosanct individuals exposed to satire. To take an exotic example: among the Ashanti of West Africa, a people so sensitive to ridicule that it often drives them to suicide, there is (or was recently) a festival period set apart in which even the sacred chief was satirized. "Wait until Friday," said the chief, "when the people really begin to abuse me, and if you will come and do so too it will please me." The high-priest explained to R. S. Rattray, the inquiring anthropologist, that the forebears of the Ashanti had "ordained a time, once every year, when every man and woman, free man and slave, should have freedom to speak out just what was in their head, to tell their neighbors just what they thought of them . . . [and] also the king or chief. When a man has spoken freely thus, he will feel his soul cool and quieted." [12]

To speak out on these privileged occasions is almost always to make mocking verses—in Ashanti at the *Apo* ceremony:

All is well today.
We know that a Brong man eats rats,
But we never knew that one of the royal blood eats rats.
But today we have seen our master, Ansah, eating rats.
Today all is well and we may say so, say so, say so.
At other times we may not say so, say so, say so.

In Latin at the Feast of Fools:

Gregis pastor Tityrus,
asinorum dominus,
noster est episcopus.

eia, eia, eia,
vocant nos ad gaudia
Tityri cibaria.

---

12   R. S. Rattray, *Ashanti* (Oxford: Clarendon Press, 1923), pp. 151 ff.

> *ad honorem Tityri,*
> *festum colant baculi*
> *satrapae et asini. . . .*[13]

This is David Crowne's translation:

> *We make Tityrus our pastor,*
> *Of these asses lord and master,*
> *Episcopal ecclesiaster.*
>
> *Holy smoke! delicious scents*
> *Lead us by our noses hence*
> *Where the food's in evidence.*
>
> *Granting Tityrus recognition,*
> *Men of asinine condition*
> *This feast of misrule do commission. . . .*

The uninhibited words of carnival are everywhere akin. This is the language of satire before satire becomes literature; it is preliterary as well as subliterary. These utterances are ritual gestures, marked off from real life by the parenthesis of the holiday.

It seems clear that the mechanisms behind the *Apo* ceremony of the Ashanti are very like those that prompted the festival of the Sacaea in Babylon, the Cronia in Greece, the Saturnalia and the Kalends in Rome, the Feast of Fools in France, the Lord of Misrule in England, and many other comparable rites of reversal. Diverse as the cultures concerned certainly are, the rites themselves can be brought under a single classification by an observation of Freud: "In all renunciations and limitations imposed upon the ego a periodical infringement of the prohibition is the rule; this indeed is shown by the institution of festivals, which in origin are nothing less nor more than

13. See Chambers, *Medieval Stage*, 1:320.

excesses provided by law and which owe their cheerful character to the release which they bring. The Saturnalia of the Romans and our modern carnival agree in this essential feature with the festivals of primitive people, which usually end in debaucheries of every kind and the transgression of what are at other times the most sacred commandments."[14] The festivals provide permitted release from limitation and renunciation. In the Saturnalia that release is the sanctioned way to the Golden Age. Here is a clue to what the Golden Age actually is: a time or a condition in which limitation and renunciation do not exist. This is implicit in most accounts of the Golden Age and occasionally it is made explicit.

"O happy Golden Age," exults the chorus in Samuel Daniel's translation of the famous passage from Tasso's *Aminta*; the age was happy, however, not because of milk and honey and a bountifully burgeoning earth, but because man's sexual instincts were still unrestrained, the "sweet delights of joyful amorous wights" not yet frustrated by

> That idle name of wind,
> That idol of deceit, that empty sound call'd Honor. . . .

Instead of Honor's restrictive laws, men followed

> golden laws like these
> Which Nature wrote. That's lawful which doth please.

Tasso catches here the essence of the myth.

Because all restraints are undesirable, saturnalian festivals take on their anarchic form: the slave mocks his master, the tribesman his chief; the priest burlesques the ceremony of his church. These are ritual gestures abrogating rule: the ritual satire a negative means to the positive end. In this way, it seems to me, the Golden

14. *Group Psychology and the Analysis of the Ego*, in *Standard Ed.*, ed. James Strachey (London: Hogarth Press, 1955), 18:131.

Age comes together with satire in the saturnalian festival. But the Golden Age (or Cockaigne or other versions of the Earthly Paradise) is not utopia; as we have seen it belongs to Cronus, not to Zeus. Nor is the ritual "satire" of the festival equivalent to the literary art we know. These are the elements out of which individual artists were to create their much more sophisticated structures: Thomas More and William Morris their utopias, Horace and Alexander Pope their satires. The genetic relation of the two modes, however, derives from the sanctioned license of the holiday.

It is a mighty leap from the festivals, which have the structure of ritual, to the literature of satire and utopia. In between, as it were, lie intermediate artistic forms which contain in various combinations and proportions relatively unassimilated ritualistic and mythical elements. A splendid example is the middle-Irish tale *The Vision of MacConglinne* in which the stuff of magic and folklore is used for highly sophisticated ends. The *Vision* is an epic of food, a mock-epic rather, with all the ambivalence— the longings and the mockery—we associate with tales of Cockaigne. The half-starved poet of the story lets his imagination go wild: "Then in the harbour of the lake before me I saw a juicy little coracle of beef-fat, with its coating of tallow, with its thwarts of curds, with its prow of lard, with its stern of butter. . . . Then we rowed across the wide expanse of New-Milk lake, through seas of broth, past rivermouths of mead, over swelling bois- terous waves of buttermilk, by perpetual pools of gravy."[15]

Framing this vision of Cockaigne is a structure of satire astonishing in its variety and comprehensiveness. Although the author of the *Vision* reaches into Ireland's

---

15. *Aislinge MeicConglinne*: *The Vision of MacConglinne*, trans. Kuno Meyer (London: David Nutt, 1892), p. 84.

most primitive traditions to exploit the ancient belief in magically efficacious satire, he also uses irony and ridicule and literary parody with delicacy and great sophistication. His target is nothing less than the religious and literary forms of medieval Ireland. From the most sacred Christian doctrine to the almost equally sacred heroic saga, MacConglinne's mockery spares nothing. This is a Saturnalia outside the ritual frame, a ceremony of reversal shocking and hilarious in its effect. As Robin Flower says, the *Vision* "sums up and turns into gigantic ridicule the learning of the earlier time much in the same way as François Rabelais at once typified and transcended the learning of the later Middle Ages." [16] A short step only separates *The Vision of MacConglinne*, which is compounded of primitive materials out of Cockaigne and ritual satire, from the art of Rabelais.

Some of these matters are pulled together and given point by a curious incident in the career of Francis Bacon, a man we are unlikely to think of in connection with Saturnalia, Cockaigne, and the like. In early December 1594, Bacon's mother, mindful of the holiday time to come, wrote in a letter: "I trust they will not mum nor mask nor sinfully revel at Gray's Inn." Revelry was much in the minds of those of Gray's Inn, however; and on 20 December, the twelve days of Christmas license were inaugurated by the Prince of Purpoole (in common life, Mr. Henry Holmes of Norfolk), the mock-king who with his court was to preside over the festivities. The first night's revels went well: the burlesque of court activities, the bawdy personal gibes, the parody of the administration of justice by the Crown in Council were all gaily received. Next night a performance of Shakespeare's *A Comedy of Errors* climaxed activities, but this time revelers got

16. *The Irish Tradition* (Oxford: Clarendon Press, 1947), p. 77.

out of hand and the evening ended in wild confusion. Appalled by this blow to their prestige, members of Gray's Inn asked Francis Bacon to help write an entertainment that would recoup their lost honor. On the night of 3 January, Bacon's *Gesta Grayorum; or, The History of the High and Mighty Prince Henry, Prince of Purpoole, Arch Duke of Stapulia* was performed to great applause. A character in this resolutely sober interlude begs the Prince of Purpoole to bend his mind to the conquest of nature, to undertake the "searching out, inventing, and discovering of all whatsoever is hid in secret in the world." To this end, the Prince is advised to acquire a number of aids: an enormous library; a wonderful garden, complete with birds and beasts and fish so as to provide "in a small compass a model of universal nature"; a huge cabinet containing whatever rare objects the hand of man or "the shuffle of things" has produced; and a house fitted with all instruments so as to be a palace "fit for a philosopher's stone."[17] In short, Bacon worked out in the *Gesta Grayorum* a first draft of Solomon's House, the heart of his utopia, *The New Atlantis*. Bacon's city of Bensalem is a notably chaste community, "The Virgin of the World." How remarkable it is that the conception of Solomon's House, that Cockaigne of the scientific imagination, should first have appeared in the context of a saturnalian festival.

Satire and the Golden Age are functionally linked in festival. They are associated in a different way, however, under the puzzlingly contradictory sign of the god Saturn

17. *Gesta Grayorum* is reprinted in John Nichols, *The Progresses, and Public Processions, of Queen Elizabeth*, 4 vols. (London: J. Nichols, 1788–1821), 2:1–74. On the affair, see James Spedding, *An Account of the Life and Times of Francis Bacon* (Boston: Houghton, Osgood and Company, 1878), 1:137–57.

himself. A curious doubleness has characterized Cronus-Saturn from the beginning. He has a strongly benevolent aspect insofar as he was the ruler in the Golden Age, the happiest time ever known on earth. Furthermore, after his imprisonment by Zeus, he was released, Hesiod says, to rule in the Isles of the Blest. To the Romans Saturn was the bringer of civilization to Italy, in addition to being god of agriculture and king of the Golden Age. But the other side of the myth is fearsome and dark: Cronus-Saturn castrated his father and ate his children. The sickle in the iconography of Saturn is an agricultural tool or the castrating weapon, depending upon which aspect of the myth is uppermost. He was the oldest of the gods—professionally old, Panofsky says—and when the gods came to be identified with the planets, he was associated with the slowest and most remote of all.[18] This dark side of the myth may help account for the fact that in the Middle Ages and the Renaissance Saturn is simultaneously the beneficent ruler of a paradise on earth and a singularly malignant influence on human affairs. In Chaucer's *The Knight's Tale*, "pale Saturnus the colde" boasts of his powers:

> *Myn is the drenchyng in the see so wan;*
> *Myn is the prison in the derke cote;*
> *Myn is the stranglyng and hangyng by the throte,*
> *The murmure and the cherles rebellyng,*
> *The groynynge, and the pryvee empoysonyng . . .*
> *My lookyng is the fader of pestilence.* [11.2456–69]

18. Erwin Panofsky, "Father Time," *Studies in Iconology* (New York: Oxford University Press, 1939), p. 73. For a detailed study of Saturn in the literary and pictorial traditions, see R. Klibansky, E. Panofsky, and F. Saxl, *Saturn and Melancholy* (London: Nelson, 1964).

Astrological lore regularly ascribes disasters like these, both public and personal, to Saturn. Lydgate in *The Fall of Princes* characterizes Saturn's influence in terms precisely like those above, then elsewhere in the same poem speaks of the time when Saturn, Noah, and Abraham were alive in a golden age of temperance and sobriety, when knights cherished chastity and heretics were properly punished. But Lydgate's *The Assembly of Gods* has Saturn dressed in frost and snow, holding a bloody falchion, wearing a necklace of icicles and a leaden crown.[19]

During the Renaissance in England literary satire becomes associated with the malign aspect of the Saturn character. An etymological tangle may be in part responsible. Thomas Drant in 1566 suggests the possibility that the word "satyre" may be derived from Saturn:

> *Satyre of writhled waspyshe Saturne may be namde*
> *The Satyrist must be a wasper in moode,*
> *Testie and wrothe with vice and hers, to see both blamde*
> *But courteous and frendly to the good.*
> *As Saturne cuttes of tymes with equall scythe:*
> *So this man cuttes downe synne, so coy and blythe.*[20]

Whatever the explanation, the conventional tone for English satire during the late sixteenth and early seventeenth centuries became that of cold, snarling invective. Satirists proudly speak of themselves as Saturnian men, melancholy because of his influence. Their obsessive concern with disease and death follows on the pattern of their astrological patron; in an aggressive way they are

19. In *The Fall of Princes*, see bk. 1, ll. 1815–17, 2614, 3492; bk. 7, ll. 1153–1334. In *Assembly of Gods*, see sts. 40–41, ll. 279–87.

20. Drant's poem is reprinted in Appendix A of John Peter, *Complaint and Satire in Early English Literature* (Oxford: Clarendon Press, 1956), pp. 301–2.

eager to claim for themselves his most malignant powers. Thus Renaissance satire flaunts its unpleasantly hectoring tone under the sanction of the god who in another aspect presided over the Golden Age.

When we turn from these genetic and tutelary ties to the formal relations between utopia and satire, we are on firmer ground. Aristophanes managed the conjunction superbly. Under the rule of women in the *Ecclesiazusae*, for example, all citizens are to be equal and share in wealth and pleasure:

> *mankind should possess*
> *In common the instruments of happiness.*
> *Henceforth private property comes to an end—*
> *It's all wrong for a man to have too much to spend,*
> *While others moan, starving; another we see*
> *Has acres of land tilled prosperously,*
> *While this man has not enough earth for his grave.*
> *You'll find men who haven't a single lean slave*
> *While others have hundreds to run at their call. . . .*
> *That's over: all things are owned henceforth by all.*[21]

Law courts are to be converted to banqueting halls; marriage to be abolished in favor of complete sexual freedom: "the whole city of girls are your wives now, and gratis!" In short, Praxagora, the leader of the female revolution, will rule over a hedonist's Utopia. At the same time, of course, satire pervades the play—some of it directed inward at Utopia itself (perhaps even at portions of Plato's *Republic*), but more at the follies of the real world outside. Aristophanes takes his women and their ideal state seriously. In a number of his plays—*Lysistrata, The Birds, The Clouds, Plutus*—he sets up utopian themes as a baseline from which the satire thrusts out: they form

21. Trans. Jack Lindsay, in *Complete Plays of Aristophanes*, ed. Moses Hadas (New York: Bantam Books, 1962), p. 438.

the positive term of the hilariously destructive attack.

Satire and utopia seem naturally compatible if we think of the structure of the formal verse satire, usually characterized by two main elements: the predominating negative part, which attacks folly or vice, and the understated positive part, which establishes a norm, a standard of excellence, against which folly and vice are judged. The literary utopia, on the other hand, reverses these proportions of negative and positive—as the Russian writer Eugene Zamyatin says, utopias have a plus sign—presentation of the ideal overweighing the prescriptive attack on the bad old days which Utopia has happily transcended. (It may still be true that in many utopias, Bellamy's *Looking Backward*, for example, the exposure of contemporary evils is the liveliest thing in the book.) But even without overt attack on contemporary society, utopia necessarily wears a Janus-face. The portrayal of an ideal commonwealth has a double function: it establishes a standard, a goal; and by virtue of its existence alone it casts a critical light on society as presently constituted. William Blake's *Songs of Innocence*, writes Northrop Frye, "satirize the state of experience, as the contrast which they present to it makes its hypocrisies more obviously shameful." The utopia of Rabelais's Abbey of Thélème is physically framed by negative and positive coordinates: upon the great gate of the Abbey are set fourteen verses, the first seven a lively satirical catalogue of those who may not enter, the second seven a welcome to the gay, the handsome, the pure, the honest—those who are to live a life governed by the quintessential utopian injunction: "Do what thou wilt." Pantagruel, we recall, was born in Utopia.

As the next essay shows in detail, it is in Thomas More's *Utopia* itself that the two modes satire and utopia are most clearly seen to be indivisible. They share the most elemental devices of structure. Many formal verse satires, for example, are framed by an encounter between a satirist and an adversary: in one of his satires, "Horace" walks in the Forum and gets entangled in talk with an intolerable bore, or in another he goes to his learned friend Trebatius for advice and the two argue; or in his third satire "Juvenal" walks to the outskirts of Rome with the disillusioned Umbricius, while the two discuss in graphic detail the horrors of metropolitan life. In each case the encounter sets the stage for a dialogue in which the satirist attacks some target against the resistance, or at least at the prompting, of the adversary. So it is in *Utopia*. The governing fiction of the work is that Thomas More, while he was on an embassy abroad (the historical man a character in his own fiction), meets a seafaring philosopher named Raphael Hythloday. The two talk throughout a long and memorable day in a garden in Antwerp. "More's" function is to draw Hythloday out and to oppose him on certain issues, Hythloday's defense of the communism he found in the land of Utopia, for example. "More" is the adversary. Hythloday's role is to expose the corruption of contemporary society: "so God help me, I can perceive nothing but a certain conspiracy of rich men procuring their own commodities under the name and title of the commonwealth" and to set up against that corruption a norm: the picture of an ideal commonwealth, Utopia, "which alone of good right may take upon it the name." Hythloday is a satirist— a magnificent satirist, commanding the entire range of tones and rhetorical techniques available to his kind. He makes lavish use of his talent.

Just as satire is a necessary element of the work which gave the literary form "utopia" its name, so, I should think, the utopias of Lilliput, Brobdingnag, and Houyhnhnmland are essential to the satire of More's great follower, Jonathan Swift. I suspect that we distinguish between *Utopia* as "a utopia" and *Gulliver's Travels* as "a satire" primarily because of the difference in distribution of positive and negative elements in the two works. Both are necessary to both kinds.

To summarize: utopia is the secularization of the myth of the Golden Age, a myth incarnated in the festival of the Saturnalia. Satire is the secular form of ritual mockery, ridicule, invective—ritual gestures which are integrally part of the same festival. Thus utopia and satire are ancestrally linked in the celebration of Saturn, a god who reigns over the earthly paradise, but who also by reason of his concern with melancholy, disease, and death becomes the patron of snarling Renaissance satirists. The two modes are formally joined in More's eponymous work, and indeed the very notion of utopia necessarily entails a negative appraisal of present conditions. Satire and utopia are not really separable, the one a critique of the real world in the name of something better, the other a hopeful construct of a world that might be. The hope feeds the criticism, the criticism the hope. Writers of utopia have always known this: the one unanswerable argument for the utopian vision is a hard satirical look at the way things are today.

2

The Shape of Utopia

More's Utopians are a peace-loving people, but their land was born to controversy. Many claim it: Catholics and Protestants, medievalists and moderns, socialists and communists; and a well-known historian has recently turned it over to the Nazis. Methods of legitimating claims vary widely, although most are necessarily based upon ideological interpretations of More's book. Over the past generation, however, in all the welter of claim and counter-claim, one single interpretation has emerged to dominate the field. H. W. Donner calls it "the Roman Catholic interpretation" of *Utopia*.[1] Its most trenchant, certainly most influential, statement is by R. W. Chambers; the interpretation, in brief, amounts to this: "When a Sixteenth-Century Catholic

1. *Introduction to Utopia* (London: Sidgwick & Jackson, 1945), p. 81.

depicts a pagan state founded on Reason and Philosophy, he is not depicting his ultimate ideal. . . . The underlying thought of *Utopia* always is, *With nothing save Reason to guide them, the Utopians do this; and yet we Christian Englishmen, we Christian Europeans . . .!*" [2] This statement cuts cleanly through murky tangles of critical debate. It is founded upon awareness of the relation between reason and revelation in Catholic doctrine, and the importance of that relation in making judgments about *Utopia*; it is consonant with everything we know of More and his life. Most recently this interpretation has received powerful support from Edward L. Surtz, S.J., in a number of articles and in two books he has written on More's *Utopia: The Praise of Pleasure* (Cambridge: Harvard University Press, 1957) and *The Praise of Wisdom* (Chicago: Loyola University Press, 1957). Father Surtz begins and ends both books with versions of the Chambers thesis, which he too calls "the 'Catholic' interpretation of *Utopia*." [3]

The interpretation itself seems to me unassailable, the way of labeling it open to question. How far, one is bound to ask, does acceptance of this "Catholic" reading entail the acceptance of other Catholic interpretations which may seem corollary? The problem arises as one reads the work of Father Surtz. In the preface to *The Praise of Wisdom*, Father Surtz announces that his intention is to "produce additional evidence, throw more light, modify present interpretations, and draw new conclusions on intriguing but vexing problems." The book and its companion volume fulfill splendidly this aim. But it is also true that in both books Father Surtz arrives at

2. Raymond W. Chambers, *Thomas More* (London: J. Cape, 1935), p. 128.

3. "Interpretations of *Utopia*," *Catholic Historical Review* 38 (1952): 168 and n. 52.

Catholic interpretations of various issues in *Utopia* which seem to me—and, I would assume, to a good many others—quite unacceptable. One admires the frankness with which he admits the perplexities, even the irritations, he has encountered in dealing with prickly religious and moral sentiments expressed in *Utopia*, but one cannot accept—even as satisfactory explanation—the way he has dealt with some of them.

To be specific: the Utopians notoriously recommend euthanasia for the incurably ill. There is no equivocation on this point in the text. As Raphael Hythloday reports matters, the Utopians believe that a man whose life has become torture to himself will be—and should be—glad to die; in these extreme cases the priests and magistrates exhort the patient to take his own life. Responding to this passage, Father Surtz deals roundly with the Utopians: they "need to be set straight by Christian revelation on this point." Similarly, some Utopians "err," he writes, "in the maintenance of an extreme view of immortality," for they think the souls of even brute animals are immortal. Because divorce is allowed in Utopia, Father Surtz scolds the inhabitants for violating the natural law "which is obligatory on all men, Christian and non-Christian, including the Utopians." Mistakes like these would have become evident to the Utopians had they "been fortunate enough to possess supernatural revelation." [4]

This way of dealing with religious questions in Utopia is not only to number Lady Macbeth's children but to spank them as well. Perhaps it is a tribute to More's creative powers that Father Surtz should treat the Utopians as though they were subject to judgments of the same order as persons who actually live. "In his heart,"

4. *Praise of Wisdom*, pp. 91, 77–78, 247, 11.

he writes of Raphael Hythloday and his attitude toward
Utopian communism, "he realizes that, given the general
run of Christians, his commonwealth, like the republic of
Plato, will never exist in the Christian West."[5] But
Hythloday has no heart: as Dr. Johnson says, trees
conjured up by the imagination are not capable of pro-
viding us shade. It is no good looking behind Hythloday's
words to concealed or unacknowledged meanings: Hythloday *is* only the words that the words of Thomas More
say he speaks. Father Surtz's argument against Hythloday on Utopian communism is undoubtedly cogent from
a doctrinal point of view, but it has little to do with the
literary work in which the ideas on communism exist.

The major problem is one of method. Father Surtz
seeks to discover More's "real intent and thought."
In the last chapter of *The Praise of Pleasure* he writes that
his method is "to study each problem by itself in the
light of all [More's] letters and writings and against the
background of antecedent and contemporary literature and
philosophy." In the preface to *The Praise of Wisdom* he
says that he examines the "pertinent sections in the
Utopia point by point . . . to determine the relation of
each point to fifteenth-century and sixteenth-century
formulations of Catholic teaching." The method provides
us with an admirable historical, philosophical, and religious
context for the many vexed issues that arise in *Utopia*.
Three chapters on communism in *The Praise of Pleasure*,
for example, afford a comprehensive account of classical,
scriptural, patristic, and humanist attitudes toward the
matter. All the major issues of *Utopia* are thus "placed."
We are given no sense, however, that these questions exist,
not as abstract political, religious, or philosophical proposi-
tions, but as constitutive elements in a work of art. What is

5. *Praise of Pleasure*, p. 181.

wanted instead of the Catholic interpretation of communism
is an interpretation of *Utopia* that will show us how the question of communism is incorporated into the total structure of
the work. Father Surtz is aware of a problem of literary
interpretation; he recognizes the ironic structure of
Utopia—in fact, he deplores it. "Unfortunately," he
writes, "for purposes of satire or irony [More] has
introduced into his 'philosophical city' institutions which
impart an air of realism but which he himself terms silly
or even absurd. Correct interpretation becomes trouble-
some and elusive."[6] The *Utopia*, by virtue of what it *is*,
becomes an obstacle to Father Surtz's purpose. Something
is radically wrong.

Clearly we need, not the Catholic or the Marxist or the
city-planner interpretation of *Utopia*, so much as we
need an interpretation that will tell us what *Utopia* is, that
will place it with respect to the literary conventions which
give it form and control its meaning. In one sense, of
course, *Utopia* made its own conventions: it is the beginning, it creates its own genre. More was like Adam in the
Garden of Eden: his use of the name was constitutive; he
named the thing and that is what it was.

But in another sense the Adamic form was hardly new
at all. Its structure, its use of characters, its rhetorical
techniques, its purpose, its subject, its tone—all these
have much in common with the conventions of a literary
genre firmly, if ambiguously, fixed in literary history.
Utopia has the shape and the feel—it has much of the
form—of satire. It is useful to think of it as a prose version
with variations of the formal verse satire composed by
Horace, Persius, and Juvenal. If we approach it in this
way, we shall be able to adjust our expectations and our

6. *Praise of Pleasure*, p. 193.

ways of interpreting and evaluating to conform to the laws of the country to which *Utopia* belongs.[7]

We can establish the general shape of *Utopia* by putting together two comments of More's contemporaries. "If you have not read More's Utopia," writes Erasmus to his friend William Cop, "do look out for it, whenever you wish to be amused, or rather I should say, if you ever want to see the sources from which almost all the ills of the body politic arise." The second comment is from Jerome Busleyden's letter to More, published with the *Utopia*: You have done the whole world inestimable service, he writes, "by delineating . . . an ideal commonwealth, a pattern and finished model of conduct, than which there has never been seen in the world one more wholesome in its institution, or more perfect, or to be thought more desirable."[8] Here are the two sides of *Utopia*: the negative, which exposes in a humorous way the evils affecting the body politic; the positive, which provides a normative model to be imitated. "O holy commonwealth, which Christians ought to emulate" (*O sanctam rempublicam, et uel Christianis imitandam*) reads a marginal comment on the text by either Erasmus or Peter Giles.

7. Cf. A. R. Heiserman, "Satire in the *Utopia*," *PMLA* 78 (1963): 163–74.

8. Epistle 519 in *The Epistles of Erasmus*, trans. Francis M. Nichols (New York: Russell & Russell, 1962), 2:503; *Utopia*, ed. J. H. Lupton (Oxford: Clarendon Press, 1895), p. 315. I have used the Lupton edition for both the Latin text·and the ancillary material published with *Utopia*. For the English text of *Utopia* itself I use the modernized spelling version of the Ralph Robynson translation (originally published 1551) issued by Everyman Library, 1951. Since this essay was written, the Yale *Utopia* has appeared (1965), edited by Father Surtz and J. H. Hexter; it contains the Latin text, a translation based on that of G. C. Richards (1923), introductions, full apparatus, and notes. The translation, edited by Father Surtz, is also available in a Yale paperback (1964).

This general negative-positive structure is of course common enough in many forms of discourse. Saint Augustine very consciously organized *The City of God* this way: the first ten books attacking erroneous beliefs, the last twelve establishing his own position, with destructive and constructive elements working through both parts. Sermons are often put together on this principle, as are literary-moral forms like the beast fable in which the greedy fox comes to a bad and instructive end. But for our purposes it is significant that this too is the characteristic skeletal shape of the formal verse satire as it was written by Horace, Persius, and Juvenal. The Roman satire divides readily into two disproportionate elements: part A (as Mary Claire Randolph has called it) in which some aspect of man's foolish or vicious behavior is singled out for exposure and dissection, and part B, which consists (whether explicitly or implicitly) of an admonition to virtue and rational behavior.[9] It establishes the standard, the "positive," against which vice and folly are judged.

Utopia and Roman satire have in common this general structural outline, as well as many other canonical elements. So true is this that one must read the *Utopia* with an eye—and an ear—to complexities of the kind one finds in Horace and Alexander Pope, testing the voices of the speakers against the norms of the work, weighing each shift of tone for possible moral implication. The meaning of the work as a whole is a function of the way those voices work

9. "The Structural Design of the Formal Verse Satire," *PQ* 21 (1942):368–74. Cf. A. Cartault: "Les satires morales d'Horace contiennent une partie de destruction et une partie de construction; en d'autres termes une partie satirique et une partie proprement morale. Ce sont deux faces de la même oeuvre, mais elles sont étroitement soudées entre elles; on peut les distinguer, non les séparer." *Etude sur les Satires d'Horace* (Paris: F. Alcan, 1899), p. 347.

with and against each other: a function of the pattern they form.

More knew ancient satire well. Lucian was one of his favorite authors: "If . . . there was ever anyone who fulfilled the Horatian precept and combined delight with instruction, I think Lucian certainly stood *primus inter pares* in this respect," he wrote in the dedicatory epistle prefacing the translation into Latin of some of Lucian's dialogues on which he and Erasmus collaborated.[10] He often quoted from the Latin satirists, and it is clear that he had given a good deal of thought to certain problems having to do with satire as a form. When the Louvain theologian Martin Dorp attacked Erasmus's *Praise of Folly*, More replied in a long letter in which he defends the *Folly* with arguments drawn from the *apologiae* of the Roman satirists and from Saint Jerome's justification of his own satire. More's letter, together with the dedicatory essay to him in the *Praise of Folly* and Erasmus's own epistolary *apologia* written to the same Martin Dorp (who in real life played the conventional role of the *adversarius* in satire), form an elaborate compendium of arguments satirists have always used to justify their ambiguous art.[11]

10. Translation by C. R. Thompson in his *The Translations of Lucian by Erasmus and St. Thomas More* (Ithaca, N.Y. [Binghamton, N.Y.: The Vail-Ballou Press], 1940), pp. 24–25.

11. For a study of the conventional *apologia*, see Lucius R. Shero, "The Satirist's *Apologia*," *Classical Studies*, series no. 2, University of Wisconsin Studies in Language and Literature, no. 15 (Madison, 1922), pp. 148–67. More's letter is in *St. Thomas More: Selected Letters*, trans. Elizabeth F. Rogers (New Haven: Yale University Press, 1961), pp. 40, 42, 55–61. Erasmus's letter is Epistle 337 in *Opus Epistolarum Des. Erasmi Roterodami*, ed. P. S. Allen and others (Oxford: Clarendon Press, 1906–58), 2:90–114. For Saint Jerome, see *Select Letters*, trans. F. A. Wright (Cambridge, Mass.: Harvard University Press, 1954), letters 22, p. 32; 40; 52, p. 17. Good discussions of Jerome as satirist are in John Peter,

As we saw in the preceding essay, *Utopia* is like many formal verse satires in that it is framed by an encounter between a satirist and an adversary. In this case "More" has the minor role, eliciting comment, prodding gently, objecting mildly, while Raphael Hythloday lays about him with the fervor of a Persius or a Juvenal. The provenance of these roles is particularly clear in the first book. At one point a query by "More" leads Hythloday into reminiscence about his stay years before with Cardinal Morton in England. He recalls a foolish argument that developed at table one day between a jesting scoffer who was accustomed to play the fool and an irascible friar. The fool, says Hythloday, having delivered himself of some sharp gibes at the venality of monks, and finding his railing well received, made an equally sharp thrust at the friar, to the delight of the assembled company. The friar, "being thus touched on the quick and hit on the gall (*tali perfusus aceto*) so fret, so fumed, and chafed at it, and was in such a rage, that he could not refrain himself from chiding, scolding, railing, and reviling. He called the fellow ribald, villain, javel, backbiter, slanderer, and the child of perdition, citing therewith terrible threatenings out of Holy Scripture. Then the jesting scoffer began to play the scoffer indeed, and verily he was good at that. . . ." The climax of the row came when the friar threatened to invoke the curse of Elisha against the fool and to excommunicate him. With that, Cardinal Morton intervened, says Hythloday, to end the grotesque little episode.

Hythloday apologizes twice for telling this story; and although it has some slight relevance to Hythloday's

Complaint and Satire in Early English Literature (Oxford: Clarendon Press, 1956), pp. 15 ff.; David S. Wiesen, *St. Jerome as a Satirist* (Ithaca, N.Y.: Cornell University Press, 1964).

major theme and a burlesque-show quality of humor about it, it is not immediately apparent why More includes it. Certain elements in the scene, however—the spiraling invective, the character of contest and performance, of flyting, and the threat of a fatal curse—these are the primitive stuff from which formal satire developed: the underwood of satire, Dryden called it.[12] But in addition to genetic sanctions, More had excellent literary precedent. The scene is modeled on Horace's *Satires* 1. 7, which consists largely of a contest in scurrility between a witty half-Greek trader and a "foul and venomous" Roman. (It is also very like the wit-contest in *Satires* 1. 5 ["The Journey to Brundisium"] between Sarmentus the jester and the buffoon Messius Cicirrus, which so delighted the distinguished characters in the poem—Horace himself, Maecenas, and Virgil.) A marginal note to the Latin text of *Utopia* calls attention to More's use of the phrase *perfusus aceto* from Horace's satire, and thus makes explicit the relation between the two scenes. Horace's poem ends with a pun, More's episode with the discomfiture of the foolish friar. His satire is the sharper.

Immediately before this scene Hythloday had been engaged (he tells "More" and "Giles") in a more serious contest with a lawyer at Cardinal Morton's table. The lawyer praised the rigors of English justice which loads twenty thieves at a time on one gallows. Hythloday, radically disagreeing, attacked the severity of the punishment and the social conditions which drive men to theft. A single passage from this dialogue-within-a-dialogue is enough to establish Hythloday's superb talent as satirist.

12. "Essay on Satire," *Works*, ed. Scott, Saintsbury (Edinburgh: W. Paterson, 1882–93), 13:47. For discussion of the primitive materials out of which literary satire grew, see Robert C. Elliott, *The Power of Satire: Magic, Ritual, Art* (Princeton: Princeton University Press, 1960), chaps. 1, 2, and pp. 158–59.

He speaks:

> There is another [necessary cause of stealing], which, as I
> suppose, is proper and peculiar to you Englishmen alone.
>   What is that? quoth the cardinal.
>   Forsooth, my lord, quoth I, your sheep that were wont
> to be so meek and tame and so small eaters, now, as I hear
> say, be become so great devourers and so wild, that they
> eat up and swallow down the very men themselves. They
> consume, destroy, and devour whole fields, houses, and
> cities. For look in what parts of the realm doth grow the
> finest and therefore dearest wool, there noblemen and
> gentlemen, yea and certain abbots, holy men no doubt, not
> contenting themselves with the yearly revenues and profits
> that were wont to grow to their forefathers and predecessors
> of their lands, nor being content that they live in rest and
> pleasure nothing profiting, yea, much annoying the
> weal-public, leave no ground for tillage. They enclose all
> into pastures; they throw down houses; they pluck down
> towns, and leave nothing standing but only the church to
> be made a sheep-house.[13]

Here are characteristic devices of the satirist, dazzlingly
exploited: the beast fable compressed into the grotesque
metaphor of the voracious sheep; the reality-destroying
language which metamorphoses gentlemen and abbots
into earthquakes, and a church into a sheep barn; the
irony coldly encompassing the passion of the scene. Few
satirists of any time could improve on this.

   Hythloday is expert in his role, which means, of course,
that More is expert in his. It does not mean that More's
satire and his values are identical with those of the character he created. The interesting and delicate critical question
throughout *Utopia* is to determine where possible the
relation between the two. To what degree does Thomas

13. Marx quoted the passage in *Capital*: see the translation of the
3d edition by Samuel Moore and Edward Aveling (New York:
Modern Library, 1906), p. 791 n.

More share in the negative criticism of Raphael Hythloday and in the standards of excellence (part B of Hythloday's satire) which from time to time he voices? The problem seems to be simplified by the fact that More is himself a character—a real character in a real garden—in the dialogue; he argues with Hythloday, agrees with many things he says, disagrees with others, and in general conducts himself in such a way that we inevitably tend to identify "More" with More, the sentiments uttered by "More" in the dialogue in the garden with those actually held by the emissary from London. "For, when, in any dialogue," writes R. W. Chambers, "More speaks in his own person, he means what he says. Although he gives the other side a fair innings, he leaves us in no doubt as to his own mind."[14] A great many critics have agreed with Chambers.

It is a dangerous assumption. More dealt habitually in irony: Beatus Rhenanus once characterized him as "every inch pure jest,"[15] and no one in life knew quite how to take him. "But ye use . . . to loke so sadly when ye mene merely," More has a friend say in a dialogue, "that many times men doubte whyther ye speke in sporte, when ye mene good ernest."[16] To assume that he could not be similarly mercurial in *Utopia* is unreasonable. Lucian and Horace, appearing as characters in their own dialogues, sometimes come croppers themselves, end up

14. *More*, p. 155.

15. Thomas More, *Latin Epigrams*, trans. Leicester Bradner and Charles A. Lynch (Chicago: University of Chicago Press, 1953), p. 126. More suppressed this characterization (which appears in the letter prefacing the Epigrams) in the 3d edition of 1520; see *Epigrams*, p. xvi.

16. "A Dialogue Concernynge Heresyes," *English Works*, ed. William Rastell (London: Cawod, Waly & Tottell, 1557), p. 127.

as butts of their own satire. More's capacities are similar. I see no way of resolving the cruxes in *Utopia* which have caused so much controversy except by avoiding a priori judgments and listening to the voices as they speak.

In the governing fiction of *Utopia* "More" is much taken with his new friend whose eloquence is remarkably persuasive; but on two major matters they disagree, and in book 1 they argue their respective positions. The points at issue are, first, "More's" conviction that it is the duty of a philosopher like Hythloday to take service in a prince's court so that his wise counsel may benefit the commonwealth; and, second, Hythloday's contention that "where possessions be private, where money beareth all the stroke, it is hard and almost impossible that there the weal-public may justly be governed and prosperously flourish"—in short, his argument for communism. Neither argument is conclusive in book 1, but for different reasons.

The Dialogue of Counsel (as J. H. Hexter calls it) is inconclusive because opponents, arguments, and rhetoric are evenly matched.[17] In many formal satires the interlocutor is a mere mechanism, set up to launch opinions for the satirist to shoot down. Not so here. "More" invokes Platonic doctrine as he urges upon Hythloday his duty to join the court of a king. Hythloday responds by creating hypothetical examples showing the folly of a moral man's attempting to influence the immoral counsels which prevail at European courts. But, says "More," a sense of decorum is necessary: counsel tempered to the possibilities available, the ability to take a part in the play actually in hand. "You must not forsake the ship in a tempest because you cannot rule and keep down the winds . . . you must with a crafty wile and a subtle train

17. *More's Utopia* (Princeton: Princeton University Press, 1952), pp. 99–138.

study and endeavour yourself, as much as in you lieth, to handle the matter wittily and handsomely for the purpose; and that which you cannot turn to good, so to order it that it be not very bad. For it is not possible for all things to be well unless all men were good, which I think will not be yet this good many years."

Against the realism of this, which urges the moral man to work for the limited good possible in a wicked world, Hythloday poses his intransigent idealism: "if I would speak such things that be true I must needs speak such things; but as for to speak false things, whether that be a philosopher's part or no I cannot tell, truly it is not my part." The satirist has always maintained that he must blurt out the truth, whatever the cost.[18]

Both arguments are coherent, eloquent, persuasive; they meet head-on, as they were to meet 150 years later in the confrontation of Alceste and Philinte in Molière's *Misanthrope*; as they were to meet 450 years later, with total "relevance," in countless confrontations over the grave political-moral issues of the 1960s. History provides no certain conclusion to the dialogue. From the text of *Utopia* itself it is impossible to say who "wins" in the Dialogue of Counsel. Not long after writing it, More took service with Henry VIII; possibly he composed the argument as a move in a complex political game; or perhaps we had better think of it, with David Bevington, as a dialogue of More's mind with itself.[19] In any case, More's action in life has no necessary bearing on the debate conducted so brilliantly in the hypothetical realm of his book.

18. Cf. Horace, *Satires*, 2. 1. 1. 59; Persius, *Satires*, 1. 1. 120; Juvenal, *Satires*, 1. 11. 30, 79.

19. "The Dialogue in Utopia," *SP* 58 (1961):495–509.

The argument over communism is inconclusive in book 1 for a different reason. Hythloday claims the authority of Plato when he says that only if all things are held in common can a justly governed and prosperous commonwealth be established. "More" disagrees and in four bare sentences advances the classical objections to communism: it destroys initiative, encourages dependence on others and hence sloth, is conducive to sedition, bloodshed, and the destruction of authority. But, responds Hythloday (in the perennially effective gambit of utopian fiction), you have not seen Utopia! If you had lived there for five years as I did, "you would grant that you never saw people well ordered but only there." A good deal of book 2 is, in effect, an answer to "More's" objections; and in this sense the dialogue continues, to be concluded only at the end of the tale.

Throughout book 1 Raphael Hythloday's concentration is on those things which, in Erasmus's words, cause commonwealths to be less well off than they should be; this is consistent with his role as satirist. He exposes evil, bares the sources of corruption, as in his Juvenalian outburst against "that one covetous and insatiable cormorant and very plague of its native country," who may enclose thousands of acres of land, forcing the husbandmen and their families out onto the road, into beggary, theft, thence to the gallows. Hythloday attacks fiercely, but as he opens up one social problem after another he suggests remedies, balancing off the negative criticism with positive suggestion. On the enclosure question he exhorts to action: "Cast out these pernicious abominations; make a law that they which plucked down farms and towns of husbandry shall re-edify them. . . . Suffer not these rich men to buy up all to engross and forestall, and with their monopoly to keep the market alone as please them. Let . . . husbandry and tillage be restored. . . ." In the argument with the lawyer over the treatment of thieves ("What can they then else do but steal, and then justly pardy be hanged?"), he recommends for England the ways of the Polylerites, which he describes in detail. Within one frame of reference these are the positives—the norms—of Hythloday the satirist; and as they seem convincing to "Cardinal Morton," we have good reason to believe that Thomas More approves.

Hythloday realizes, however, that these positives, important as they may be in the circumstances of the moment, are mere palliatives. In his view, as long as private property exists it will be impossible to remove from "among the most and best part of men the heavy and inevitable burden of poverty and wretchedness." To be sure, mitigating laws can be passed, and he lists a number of possibilities; but this would be only to "botch up for a time" a desperately sick body; no cure is possible "whiles every man is master of his own to himself." Hythloday is no man for half measures; his true positive, the standard to which he is passionately committed, is that of full cure. The necessary condition of cure in his view is community of property. "More," we know, flatly disagrees, and the burden of proof is left to Hythloday. Book 2 is the statement of his case.

The statement is largely expository and, until the very end, notably undramatic (an unhappy characteristic of most comparable statements, obligatory in subsequent literary utopias). Book 2 is still satiric, as we shall see, but it is as though the normal proportions of satire were here reversed, with part B—the positives—in preponderance. Hythloday makes some pretense of being objective in his discussion of the institutions of Utopia ("we have taken upon us to shew and declare their laws and ordinances, and not to defend them"), but his enthusiasm overwhelms objectivity. Only occasionally does he express any reservation, as when he remarks that the Utopians seem almost too much inclined to the opinions of those who place the felicity of man in pleasure (but then "pleasure" is scrupulously and favorably defined), or as when he and his fellows laugh at the custom according to which a Utopian wooer and his lady see each other naked before marriage. Although Hythloday finds this a "fond and foolish" practice, the arguments advanced by the Utopians (as reported by Hythloday) are most persuasive, so that the thrust of the rhetoric in the passage favors the custom, while Hythloday condemns it. This is a clear point at which the norms of the work itself are not in accord with Hythloday's standards. His disclaimer works as a double ironic shield for Thomas More: "I am not Hythloday, and besides he is against it; he says so." Still, *Utopia* argues for the practice.[20]

Except for this, however, Hythloday's tale is of a realm that he finds ideal, where laws, customs, and institutions are designed to foster the good, and to suppress the wickedness, in man. Utopians are not perfect people, but their commonwealth is rationally conducted so that in nearly every point of comparison the Utopian achievement is a reproach to the nations of Europe. Chambers's comment is worth repeating: "The underlying thought

20. The *Utopia* is a textbook on the use of irony as protective device. "Utopia" ("nowhere"), "Hythloday" ("purveyor of nonsense")—many of the place names bearing comparable significance act as formal disclaimers encompassing the harsh truths told in the work. More's second letter to Peter Giles (Yale *Utopia*, p. 251) points this up. In "A Dialogue Concernynge Heresyes," More mocks some of these devices while elaborately using them: "More" is discussing problems of heresy with the messenger from a friend. The messenger insists that what he says is not his opinion but what he has heard others say. But "More" forgets: "And first wher ye say. Nay quod he where thei say. Well quod I, so be it, where they say. For here euer my tong trippeth." *English Works*, ed. Rastell, p. 124.

of *Utopia* always is, *With nothing save Reason to guide them, the Utopians do this; and yet we Christian Englishmen, we Christian Europeans . . .!"* In this sense the very presentation of Utopian life has a satiric function insofar as it points up the discrepancy between what is and what ought to be.

Hythloday has so much explanation to get through in book 2 that the expository tone necessarily dominates his discourse. Still, that preoccupation does not force him to abandon his role as overt satirist. At times, while discussing the way of life of the Utopians he thinks of Europe and becomes hortatory, as though preaching to an audience rather than addressing "More" or "Giles." What shall I say, he asks, of misers who hide their gold? "And whiles they take care lest they shall lose it, do lose it indeed. For what is it else, when they hide it in the ground, taking it both from their own use and perchance from all other men's also? And yet thou, when thou hast hid thy treasure, as one out of all care hoppest for joy" (*et tu tamen abstruso thesauro, uelut animi iam securus, laetitia gestis*). We are not to think here of "More" or "Giles" dancing in delight after digging his gold into the ground; the shift in person is to the indefinite "thou" (*tu*) of an audience "out there." Passages like these have the feel of medieval complaint, although in the sudden shift of person and the moralistic utterance they are completely in character with many Roman satires: some of Persius', for example, or Horace's *Satires* 2. 3. 11. 122 ff. which is on exactly the same theme.

Hythloday sounds another variation on the satirist's tone when he speaks of the extraordinary learning of the Utopians who, without having heard of the Greeks, knew all that the Greeks knew of music, logic, and mathematics. "But," he adds, "as they in all things be almost equal to our old ancient clerks, so our new logicians in subtle

inventions have far passed and gone beyond them. For
they have not devised one of all those rules of restrictions,
amplifications, and suppositions, very wittily invented in
the small logicals which here our children in every place do
learn." The voice is suddenly that of the ingénu, of Gulliver
speaking two hundred years before his time, but with this
difference: Gulliver would believe what he said, whereas
Hythloday is ironic.

He can use the technique lightly, as above, or with a
bitter, driving, daring intensity. He is explaining that the
Utopians do not enter into treaties with their neighbors
because treaties are often broken in their part of the
world. It is not so in Europe, says Hythloday: "especially
in these parts where the faith and religion of Christ
reigneth, the majesty of leagues is everywhere esteemed
holy and inviolable, partly through the justice and goodness of princes, and partly at the reverence and motion of
the head bishops. Which, like as they make no promise
themselves but they do very religiously perform the same,
so they exhort all princes in any wise to abide by their
promises, and them that refuse . . . they compel thereto.
And surely they think well that it might seem a very
reproachful thing if, in the leagues of them which by a
peculiar name be called faithful, faith should have no
place." Again, the echoes set up in one's ears are from a
later traveler to Utopia, whose praise of things European
withers what it touches. Gulliver's predecessor, Hythloday, is using with exemplary skill the ancient rhetorical
trick of blame-by-praise. As Alexander Pope puts it:
"A vile encomium doubly ridicules."

This is superb; but the account of Utopia is enlivened
only intermittently by such flashes—or by sudden bits
of internal dialogue, so characteristic of Roman satire,
like that between the mother and child on the sumptuous
dress of the visiting Anemolians. The Utopians seem

to be a fairly sober lot, although they are delighted with the works of Lucian that Hythloday has brought with him, and (like More) they take much pleasure in fools. Their sense of the satiric is more likely to be expressed in concrete than in verbal ways: they fetter their bondsmen with chains of gold, creating thus an image of the world.

At the end of his discourse, Hythloday marshals his forces for summary and justification. Pulling together the major themes, he turns to "More" with a powerful and eloquent defense of the Utopian commonwealth ("which alone of good right may take upon it the name") and of communism ("though no man have anything, yet every man is rich"). From this he moves into outraged criticism of the ways of the world in Europe: the pampering of useless gentlemen, "as they call them," in savage contrast to the inhuman treatment of "plowmen, colliers, labourers, carters, ironsmiths, and carpenters, without whom no commonwealth can continue"; the codification of injustice into law, which is used to mulct the poor. "Therefore, when I consider and weigh in my mind all these commonwealths which nowadays anywhere do flourish, so God help me, I can perceive nothing but a certain conspiracy of rich men procuring their own commodities under the name and title of the commonwealth. They invent and devise all means and crafts, first how to keep safely, without fear of losing, that they have unjustly gathered together, and next how to hire and abuse the work and labour of the poor for as little money as may be." Christ counseled that all things be held in common, and the whole world would have come long ago to the laws of the Utopians were it not for that "one only beast, the princess and mother of all mischief, Pride."

Hythloday's tone at the end of his tale is that of prophet or hero—his final variation on the scale of tones available to the satirist. It would be idle to look for a source; many

satirists and many writers of complaint have sounded the
same trumpet: Juvenal, Saint Jerome, Piers Plowman,
great medieval preachers such as the Dominican John
Bromyard.[21]

But the heroic note is not the last note sounded. A
final paragraph remains, bracketing Hythloday's peroration, winding up the debate on communism, reasserting by
its very form the relation of *Utopia* to Roman satire—
and indeed, to a whole body of literature which distinguishes between exoteric and esoteric teaching. Nothing
could be more deft than the way "More" excuses himself
to the reader for not having voiced his objections to some
of the Utopian laws: Hythloday was tired after his long
discourse, and, besides, it was not certain he could abide
opposition. Before leading his friend into supper, "More"
contents himself with praising the Utopian institutions
and Hythloday's account of them; and in enigmatic comment he admits that while he can not agree with all that
has been said, there are many things "in the Utopian
weal-public which in our cities I may rather wish for than
hope for."

"More" leaves with us, however, a statement of the
reservations which he withheld from Hythloday—reservations about certain laws and institutions of Utopia
founded, in his view, "of no good reason" (the Latin
perquam absurde is considerably stronger). Among these
are their methods of waging war and their religious
customs, but chiefly in his mind is "the principal foundation of all their ordinances," the "community of their life
and living without any occupying of money." "More"
makes clear the grounds of his objection: by doing away
with money, "the true ornaments [*uera . . . ornamenta*]
and honours, as the common opinion is, of a common-

21. See G. R. Owst, *Literature and Pulpit in Medieval England*
(New York: Barnes & Noble, 1961), pp. 300 ff.

wealth, utterly be overthrown and destroyed." What, in "More's" view, are the true ornaments and honors of a commonwealth? They are "nobility, magnificence, worship (*splendor*), honour, and majesty." Of course we smile: while this might conceivably be Francis Bacon of *The New Atlantis* speaking, it cannot possibly be Thomas More, whose heretical opinions about magnificence are notorious.[22] This is "More," a *persona* he has created for complex purposes of his own—a *persona* who suddenly adopts the values held dear by "common opinion": the opinion which believes that nobility, magnificence, and the rest are the true ornaments of a commonwealth. But, as Father Surtz admirably says, "the whole purpose of *Utopia* has been to prove that these are *not* the qualities which should distinguish a commonwealth."[23] Unless the whole satiric thrust of *Utopia* has failed for us (as the thrust of Hythloday's discourse has apparently failed for "More"), we must recognize that at this point "More" becomes a gull.

The formal situation here is like that sometimes found in Roman satire. "More" is precisely in the case of "Horace" (*Satires* 2. 3), who, after listening in silence to Damasippus' long Stoic discourse on the theme, Everyone save the wise man is mad, loses his temper at

22. It might also be Robert Burton who, in the person of Demo-critus Junior, criticizes Plato for taking away "all splendour and magnificence" from his ideal community. Burton intends the criticism seriously. *Anatomy of Melancholy* (London: T. Tegg, 1845), pp. 58–59.

23. *Praise of Pleasure*, p. 183. Erasmus, in the wickedly witty "Julius exclusus," has Peter the Apostle identify the "ornaments" of the Church as faith, holy doctrine, contempt of the world; Pope Julius sternly corrects Saint Peter: the "true ornaments" (*vera ornamenta*) are palaces, gold, servants—everything associated with royal magnificence. The ironies parallel each other exactly.

the end, thus neatly placing himself outside the category of the sane. "Horace," like "More," is undercut by his creator.[24]

The effect of this in *Utopia* is complex. In book 1 "More" advanced cogent reasons for opposing the principle of communism advocated by Hythloday. Book 2, though it covers a good deal of ground, is fundamentally an answer to "More's" objections: Hythloday's peroration points this up. "More" remains unconvinced, but the reasons he gives, *perquam absurde*, make no sense. His disclaimer is in effect nullified by the comically ineffective way he misses the point.[25] Where does this leave us? It leaves Hythloday riding high, his arguments unanswered, his eloquence ringing in our ears. Perhaps we have been deafened a bit—or frightened. Jerome Busleyden wrote that the commonwealth of Utopia was not only an object of reverence to all nations and "one for all generations to tell of," but also "an object of fear to many."

And what of Thomas More, that man whose imagination pushed at the limits of the licit, and who wore a hair shirt? I think it very doubtful that we can ever know what he, in his many conflicting roles of philosopher, moralist,

24. Cf. Horace, *Satires*, 2. 7. More would have known the same technique in Lucian. He translated *The Cynic*, for example, in which "Lycinus" (a transparent covername for Lucian) ridicules a Cynic and ends up badly worsted in debate. (The point is not affected by the fact that Lucian's authorship of *The Cynic* is in question.)

25. Marie Delcourt, in her edition of *L'Utopie* (Paris: E. Droz, 1936), p. 207 n, says that as a precaution, "More désavoue sa propre création," although "on ne sent . . . aucune conviction réelle." A plain disavowal would have been simple; as it is, it turns back on itself. Technically, one might add, "More's" dubieties stand about the Utopians' methods of warfare, religious practices, and other laws; his disclaimer is absurd, that is, only in its application to communism.

religious polemicist, man of great affairs—what this man
"really" believed about communism.[26] Of Thomas More,
author of *Utopia*, we can speak with confidence. The idea
attracted him strongly. If by nothing else, he makes this
plain in the way that, at the climactic point of the dialogue,
he deliberately and unmistakably makes nonsense of
"More's" disclaimer. The best evidence, of course, is in
what he gives to Raphael Hythloday: the powerful criticism rooted in the realities of England; then the moral
fervor and the compelling force of his eloquence as he
argues for the institutions which make Utopia the best of
all commonwealths. In a technical sense, "More's"
early objections to communism are never met—how could
they be? Hythloday simply points to Utopia and says,
Look, it works! But we quickly forget the flimsiness of
this "proof," if we have ever noticed it, as we are swept
along by the passion of a man telling of the vision he has
seen. *Utopia* argues for the ideal of communism by the
best test available: More has given to Raphael Hythloday
all the good lines.[27]

Thus the shape of *Utopia* is finished off, enigmatically
but firmly, in the terms Hythloday provides. This reading
of the work of course conflicts with the interpretations of
Chambers, Father Surtz, and others in certain important
respects; but it need not conflict with that fundamental
position of theirs cited at the beginning of this essay:
"When a Sixteenth-Century Catholic depicts a pagan

26. For a discussion of his relevant expressions of opinion outside
Utopia, see Surtz, *Praise of Pleasure*, pp. 184–90.

27. Cf. Russell A. Ames, *Citizen Thomas More and His Utopia*
(Princeton: Princeton University Press, 1949), who says that it
should be no more necessary to prove that Hythloday speaks for
More than to prove that the King of Brobdingnag speaks for
Swift. "In general, . . . no satirist will persuasively present at
length major views with which he disagrees" (p. 37 n).

state founded on Reason and Philosophy, he is not depicting his ultimate ideal." It depends on the focus of interest. If we are more concerned with the historical Thomas More, his beliefs, his values, than we are with *Utopia* as a thing in itself, then unquestionably we must posit a norm from outside—one barely hinted at in the work. Two standards can be derived from within *Utopia* itself. The first is on the level of reform within existing institutions: laws to enforce the rebuilding of devasted farms and towns, the restriction of monopoly, provision of work for the idle, limitations on the power of the rich and the wealth of the king, and so forth. The second and higher standard is the ideal of the work itself, so to speak: Utopia, the model commonwealth, the only one worthy of the name. But if we go outside the *Utopia* for Thomas More's ideal, we must think of one far higher yet. Father Surtz cites the appropriate passage. For More, the ultimate ideal would be "the holy city, New Jerusalem, coming down out of heaven from God" (Revelation 21:2).

❦ 3 ❧

Swift's Utopias

Swift once characterized Sir Thomas More as "a person of the greatest virtue this kingdom ever produced." Perhaps he had to admire so highly before he could bring himself to imitate, the unexampled probity affording a kind of license. More's *Utopia* was a source to which Swift went repeatedly when he was writing *Gulliver's Travels*. But if Swift's attitude toward the author of *Utopia* is one of unqualified admiration, his attitude toward the idea of utopia itself is less easily stipulated.

It is true that he had the utopian temperament and an itch toward utopian solutions. He once wished that he could write a utopia for heaven, and on occasion, as in the *Project for the Advancement of Religion and the Reformation of Manners* (1709), he was willing to have a go at earth:

Among all the schemes offered to the public in this
projecting age, I have observed, with some displeasure,
that there have never been any for the improvement of
religion and morals: which, besides the piety of the
design from the consequences of such a reformation in a
future life, would be the best natural means for advancing
the public felicity of the state, as well as the present
happiness of every individual. For, as much as faith and
morality are declined among us, I am altogether confident,
they might, in a short time, and with no very great
trouble, be raised to as high a perfection as numbers are
capable of receiving. Indeed, the method is so easy and
obvious. . . .

The apparatus for bringing "this great end" about is so
repressive, the society envisaged so mean, that readers
have been tempted to absolve Swift by invoking an irony
that this time is not there. Admittedly, it shakes one to
see Swift arguing calmly the advantages of hypocrisy,
recommending that censors rewrite the literature of the
past, advocating the nominal Christianity which, in *The
Argument Against Abolishing Christianity*, written at about
the same time, he contemptuously exposes—all this and
a good deal more in the interests of raising to new heights
the levels of public felicity and private happiness. But
no discernible self-mockery undercuts this authoritarian
project: this is what Nicolas Berdyaev calls *folie raisonnante*,
the utopian temperament at work unchecked, allowing
the great end to sanction the most objectionable means.

In another early essay (*Contests and Dissensions . . . in
Athens and Rome*, 1701), Swift gravely considers, before
rejecting as beyond human power, the most utopian of
all possibilities: "Yet some physicians have thought, that
if it were practicable to keep the several humours of
the body in an exact equal ballance of each with its oppo-
site, it might be immortal; and so perhaps would a
political body, if the ballance of power could be always

held exactly even. But I doubt, this is as almost impossible in the practice as the other."

If Swift was a natural utopian, however, he was also a natural skeptic, the seemingly contrary dispositions complementing and controlling each other superbly. Understanding how a man might speculatively prefer the constitution of "an Utopia of his own" over that of his native country, he argues that "the dangers of innovation, the corruptions of mankind, and the frequent impossibility of reducing ideas to practice" would be likely to induce the speculator to join heartily in preserving the present order of things (*Examiner*, no. 29). Inevitably, Swift's satire finds a target in the utopian impulse itself, in this central disposition of his own character. A passing jibe in *The Mechanical Operation of the Spirit* equates utopian commonwealths with other objects of fanatic devotion such as the philosopher's stone and efforts to square the circle; and in *Gulliver's Travels* utopianizing in a dozen forms is submitted to the most pitiless scrutiny. Like certain undiscriminating weapons today, the satire sometimes levels far more than its ostensible target, to the puzzlement of Swift's readers. This is not, however, what causes the puzzle in Swift's first published allusion to utopia. The moral geography of the *Ode to Sir William Temple* locates virtue in "utopian ground"; Temple is exhorted to go search it out. What ironies, if any, play around this notion, I find it impossible to say.

The great test of Swift's utopian preoccupations is, of course, *Gulliver's Travels*, that salute across the centuries, R. W. Chambers called it, to Thomas More. Both More and Swift lived, as John Traugott says, with utopias in the back of their heads.[1] Utopias being the uncertain

1. Chambers, *Thomas More*, p. 365; Traugott, "A Voyage to Nowhere with Thomas More and Jonathan Swift," *Sewanee Review* 69 (1961):534–65.

things they are, however, neither man's vision could have been entirely clear, even to himself. Perhaps because they were unsure of topography and design (how wide *was* the river Anyder?), they sent their famous voyagers, Raphael Hythloday and Lemuel Gulliver, to look.

Gulliver is a splendid observer, bemused though he is by much of what he sees. No traveler has ever had more experience of utopian modes of life than he. He explores not one but many utopias, some of these in such depth that he can report on utopias within utopias, as though he were following the idea back as far as he could trace it. His exploration is conducted from the most various physical, psychological, and moral vantage points, each perspective opening up new and unexpected aspects of the object of his scrutiny. By the time he comes to write his memoirs, Gulliver is a true authority, as sure of where he stands and of what his experience means to him as is Raphael Hythloday, his great prototype. The question, of course, is what Gulliver's experience meant to Jonathan Swift.

For all his journeying, the most perfect utopia Gulliver writes of is England (unless, that is, one happens to be a horse), his own dear native country. This is the land that he celebrates, sitting in a chair perched on top of a cabinet almost at a level with the king's face, as he discourses with his Majesty of Brobdingnag. Gulliver describes a fertile island kingdom governed by a remarkable Parliament. The House of Peers is composed of men of ancient lineage and noble blood who have been prepared from childhood by the most careful education to assume their responsibilities as counsellors, legislators, judges—as faithful champions of prince and country. These lords are "the ornament and bulwark of the kingdom, worthy followers of their most renowned ancestors, whose honour had been the reward of their virtue, from which

their posterity were never once known to degenerate."
Associated with these noble men are bishops, holy persons,
Gulliver explains, in whose trust is the care of religion;
they are spiritual fathers of the people, selected by virtue
of the sanctity of their lives and the depth of their erudi-
tion. The House of Commons is made up of worthy
gentlemen "freely picked and culled out by the people
themselves, for their great abilities, and love of their
country, to represent the wisdom of the whole nation."
Venerable sages preside over courts of law, their function
to protect the innocent and punish the guilty.

For five audiences, each of several hours' duration,
Gulliver expounds the glories of this England, this
Utopia—this true no-place that has its being, as the
king quickly discovers, only in the back of Gulliver's
head. A society approaching Gulliver's vision may once
have existed, however: "I observe among you some lines
of an institution, which in its original might have been
tolerable," says the king, but corruptions have blurred
and blotted and erased those lines. Instead of the virtuous
society of Gulliver's account, which might have been
the product of that original, the king finds only an infesta-
tion of odious vermin: an appalling degeneration.

Gulliver delivers his fulsome description of utopian
England while he is a sojourner in a land that is itself a
utopia—a utopia of an entirely different order, however,
from that of Gulliver's creation. Judith Shklar's recent
comment on Brobdingnag seems to me badly misleading:

> Among the utopias that do not owe anything to classical
> antiquity at least one deserves mention here: the utopia of
> pure condemnation. Of this genre Swift is the unchallenged
> master. . . . The king of Brobdingnag, the city of giants,
> of supermen, that is, notes, after he hears Gulliver's account
> of European civilization, that its natives must be "the
> most pernicious Race of little odious Vermin that Nature

ever suffered to crawl upon the Surface of the Earth." A comparison of his utopian supra-human kingdom with those of Europe could yield no other conclusion.[2]

Brobdingnag is supra-human only in physical size, not in moral stature or political achievement; it is not an ideal, in the sense of perfect, state—by no means as ideal, for example, as the England Gulliver has pictured. (Nor, for that matter, is More's Utopia ideal in that sense— Utopia, where adultery is punished by enslavement and recalcitrant slaves are killed like wild beasts.) Brobdingnag has criminals and beggars, people of mean motives and lascivious dispositions; in the past it has been plagued with "the same disease to which the whole race of mankind is subject; the nobility often contending for power, the people for liberty, and the King for absolute dominion." Brobdingnag has progressed, however; the civil wars arising from these contentions have been brought to an end, and the government now rests securely in the equilibrium of the three estates. The situation represented here, as a number of scholars have pointed out, is Swift's version of the mixed state associated with the classical republicans, a theory of government (often confusingly called "Gothic") going back to Polybius. Swift was thoroughly familiar with the long and complex history of this mode of government. He is explicit about it in his *Contests and Dissensions . . . in Athens and Rome*, and throughout his life he remained convinced that it was the form of government best suited to accommodate and contain the disruptive forces arising from man's corrupt nature.

Thus Brobdingnag does not represent a "supra-human" kingdom in the moral and political sphere,

2. "The Political Theory of Utopia," in *Utopias and Utopian Thought*, ed. Frank Manuel (Boston: Houghton Mifflin, 1966), p. 106.

utterly beyond man's possible achievement, any more than Thomas More's picture of Utopia represents "an ideal pattern that invited contemplation and judgment but did not entail any other activity," as Professor Shklar maintains.[3] Instead of existing as objects of pure contemplation, the institutions of Utopia and Brobdingnag constitute the positive terms of severe satiric analyses of contemporary society. In both cases the satire is a call to action— sometimes specific political action. What else can Hythloday's outbursts on enclosure mean? Or the giant King's savage comments on, say, a mercenary standing army? The institutions of these "ideal" societies sanction the negative assaults and invite emulation. And if, like "More" at the end of *Utopia*, one finds many things in these societies that one may rather hope for than expect to see realized, still that hope is the justification of the satire. Even Gulliver comes to see the function of these norms. After his travels, after he has lived the good life with the horses, he allows that the Brobdingnagians are the least corrupted of Yahoos. England, he says, would do well to emulate their wise maxims in morality and government. In that sense alone Brobdingnag is an ideal society: it represents an ideal to be aimed at, a utopia with practical meaning for man.

In chapter 4 of the "Voyage to Lilliput" Gulliver announces that he has almost ready for the press a full account of the Lilliputian empire, its history, its laws and institutions, its flora and fauna, and other curious and

3. For the contrary view of Erasmus see *Utopia*, Lupton edition, p. 169. In the sixteenth century Don Vasco de Quiroga successfully established two hospital-villages in Mexico on the principles of More's Utopia. As M. Bataillon says of the venture, "Utopia did not enter here as a gratuitous fantasy, to materialize a fair dream of an artist . . . but as the only possible cure for a tragic situation." See Silvio Zavala, *Sir Thomas More in New Spain* (London: Hispanic and Luso-Brazilian Councils, 1955), p. 12.

useful matters. It is our loss that the book was never published. Nevertheless, in chapter 6 Gulliver anticipates some of the material of the projected work: he outlines for us the original utopian institutions of Lilliput. These institutions are notably highminded (the laws reward good behavior as well as punish bad; society values good morals over great abilities, etc.); they are rigid (education is strictly regulated on class lines; discipline is severe), authoritarian (the death sentence is freely pronounced, for ingratitude and fraud, as well as crimes against the state), traditional (they are closely related to those in Plato, More, and others). The institutions are also abstract, presented in a bare, almost tabular form, in contrast to the embodiment of good qualities in the people and practices of Brobdingnag: a blueprint of principles as opposed to the enactment of wise and humane behavior. Still, they are principles that appealed to the eighteenth century: the Earl of Orrery found the Lilliputian institutions an improvement on those of Lycurgus, and, with due allowance for exaggeration, Swift probably approved them himself.

The content of the utopian laws is less interesting, however, than the progeny the laws produced—a society, we recall, that reserves its honors for those who hold out longest in leaping and creeping. This shocking discrepancy between principles and practice has disturbed many readers: Sir Charles Firth speaks of a "curious contradiction," Professors Case and Quintana of inconsistency. But the contradiction is demonstrative. Swift had always an ideal of order, absolute and unchanging, as in the most fixed of utopias; but everywhere he looked he saw degeneration and corruption as central facts of life: the purity of primitive Christianity degenerating into the institutionalized idiocies of Peter and Jack; the heroes and demigods of the Roman senate degenerating into the knot of peddlars and pickpockets who made up an assembly closer to home. States are rarely ruined, wrote Swift in *Sentiments of a Church of England Man* (1708), "by any defect in their institution, but generally by the corruption of manners, against which the best institution is no long security." Thus there is no real contradiction in the treatment of Lilliput, a utopia that has lost its war with time. Given the degenerate nature of man, even the most ideal institutions will produce the corruption of the court at Belfaborac. We may find some comfort in observing, however, that at about the time when rope dancing was being introduced into Lilliput by the grandfather of the reigning emperor, the civil wars of Brobdingnag were being brought to an end by the grandfather of the king to whom Gulliver talked. The course of history, apparently, is not entirely one way.

In one part of the Academy of Lagado Gulliver encounters a reeking experimenter who for years has been trying to reduce human excrement to its original food; across the hall he witnesses the operation of a machine that enables an illiterate man to write books in philosophy by turning a crank (William Burroughs's cut-up, fold-in technique of composition owes something to the academy); but in the school of political projectors Gulliver is saddened to find a group of professors who are out of their minds:

> These unhappy people were proposing schemes for persuading monarchs to choose favourites upon the score of their wisdom, capacity and virtue; of teaching ministers to consult the public good; of rewarding merit, great abilities and eminent services; of instructing princes to know their true interest by placing it on the same foundation with that of their people: of choosing for employments persons qualified to exercise them; with many other wild impossible chimaeras, that never entered before into the heart of man to conceive. . . .

Principles held to be mad in Lagado must represent sanity to us. The proposals of the visionary professors are actually almost the same (the language is very similar) as the standards by which the king of Brobdingnag condemns the viciousness of English ways. What the king believes in and Gulliver here dismisses as impossibly utopian serves again as the positive term of the satirical attack.

This normative theme is complicated by the fact that the entire Academy of Lagado—that progenitor of negative utopias without number—is itself a "utopian" project, staffed by men like the universal artist who for thirty years has devoted all his thoughts to "the improvement of human life." The only inconvenience is, as Gulliver records, that no grass or corn grows in the fields and women rebel at the splendidly utopian effort to make the correspondence theory of language really work. Against the vision of the utopian imagination run mad, Swift shows us Lord Munodi, marooned on his splendid estate in the wastes of Balnibarbi, content "to go on in the old forms, to live in the houses his ancestors had built, and act as they did in every part of life without innovation."

Gulliver's own utopianizing bent finds its freest expression as he speculates on how he would live had he been born a *struldbrugg*: he would have gathered his brother immortals about him so that they might teach the usefulness of virtue and oppose the inroads of corruption as it steals into the world. So powerful would their influence be that they might expect to "prevent the continual degeneracy of human nature"—a utopian ambition of staggering magnitude. Gulliver's disillusion is in proportion, as he learns the rules of the hideous game of immortality.

Thus Gulliver's experiences on his third voyage subject him to a good many manifestations of the utopian spirit:

the misapplication of the intellect in a restive search for the good of man; the retreat to an ideal past where the old forms survive precariously amid compulsive experiment; the "insane" projects of political speculators which accord with the policies and values institutionalized in Brobdingnag; the pleasing vision of immortality become nightmare. After such experience, what hope?

Among the Houyhnhnms Gulliver experiences utopia in all its purity and all its power. It is exceptionally pure, a pastoral utopia of great simplicity and asceticism, established on an economic base, as A. L. Morton says, roughly that of the Neolithic age. The Houyhnhnms have no clothing, do not know the use of metals; they have no words for law or government; they have no history. They lead lives of rational benevolence and effortless virtue, enlivened by their interest in poetry and athletics. The experience of a mode of life wholly rational, virtuous, beautiful is overwhelming for Gulliver; he embraces it with all his capacity, and he rejects his own kind forever. Gulliver has found the ideal for which his travels have prepared him.

It is, of course, a curious ideal, and it is most perplexing to try to determine what the ideal is ideal in respect to. Are we to take it that Gulliver's murderous crew marooned him in a utopia that has the kind of meaning for man that, say, More's Utopia has, with its concrete suggestions of reform, its model commonwealth not altogether beyond the capacity of man to achieve? Or are we to take it as Socrates tells us to take the Republic:

> I understand, said Glaucon: you mean this commonwealth we have been founding in the realm of discourse; for I think it nowhere exists on earth.
> No, I replied; but perhaps there is a pattern set up in the heavens for one who desires to see it and, seeing it, to found one in himself. But whether it exists anywhere

or ever will exist is no matter; for this is the only
commonwealth in whose politics he can ever take part.

This, comments Northrop Frye, "is not a dream to be
realized in practice; it is an informing power in the
mind."[4] Whether any given utopia is to be thought of as
realizable for man or not depends upon the degree of
ideality of the utopia and upon what one thinks of man's
capacities for good and evil. A function of utopia is to
put the question: what is man? and what can he become?

Professor Ronald S. Crane demonstrated how concretely
that question was in Swift's mind when he wrote *Gulliver's
Travels*.[5] Swift's point of reference was the ancient
definition of man that had become a cliché in the textbooks of logic of the seventeenth century. As the Dutch
logician Burgersdyck expresses it: "Man feels, a Plant
not: But a Horse *also feels*, and likewise other Beasts.
Divide we therefore Animate Corporeal Feeling Substance
into Rational and Irrational. Here therefore *are we to
stand*, since it appears that every, and only Man *is
Rational*." Or, as a great many others say it less painfully: *Homo est animal rationale*.

Swift tests the definition in a thoroughly characteristic
way, breaking it down into its constituent parts, submit-
ting each part to intense pressure. "I . . . demand the
liberty," he once wrote, "of putting the case as strongly
as I please." His superb literalizing imagination loads
the phrase *animal rationale* with as much meaning as it will
bear. For the term *animal* he presents the quintessential

4. "Varieties of Literary Utopias," *Utopias and Utopian Thought*,
p. 34.
5. "The Houyhnhnms, the Yahoos, and the History of Ideas,"
in *Reason and the Imagination*, ed. J. A. Mazzeo (New York:
Columbia University Press, 1962), pp. 231–53. It is interesting to
compare this' theme in Cyrano de Bergerac's *L'Autre Monde*,
which strongly influenced Swift.

representative of the class—as Crane shows, the representative used repeatedly by logicians to point up the contrast between *animal* and *homo*: the horse, the brute characterized by the *facultas hinniendi*. What horses, in Swift's hands, they are! For the term *rationale* he presents reason pure and uncorrupted, a faculty that does not allow of opinions or disputes, but leads immediately to certitude. By this faculty the Houyhnhnms are wholly governed and from this faculty derives the unembattled moral tenor of their lives. Here, in an unscrupulously concrete representation, is the *animal rationale*, with each whinny refuting the logicians' definition of man.

A good many alternative definitions are offered in *Gulliver's Travels*, all strikingly similar to each other, all supported by an appalling amount of evidence. The good King of Brobdingnag defines man as an odious vermin. The Houyhnhnms define him as a Yahoo endowed with enough reason to make him more vicious, more dangerous, more contemptible than the brutes of their own land. Gulliver's definition is in complete accord: "When I thought of my family, my friends, my countrymen, or human race in general, I considered them as they really were, Yahoos in shape and disposition, only a little more civilized, and qualified with the gift of speech, but making no other use of reason than to improve and multiply those vices whereof their brethren in this country had only the share that nature allotted to them." Even the Yahoos add their own inarticulate definition when a black-haired female nearly rapes the hapless Gulliver. To say that *Gulliver's Travels* as a whole defines man in these absolute terms, however, would be an oversimplification. Clearly it makes a black joke of *homo est animal rationale*; but at the same time it subverts the alternative formula, man is a Yahoo, by presenting concrete evidence about man that the formula cannot accommodate. Glumdalclitch, the giant king, Don Pedro de Mendez, even the long-suffering Mrs. Lemuel Gulliver—these people are not vermin, they are not filthy brutes, they do not use their reason only to multiply their vices. On the contrary, by their actions, by the quality of their lives, this saving remnant calls into question the adequacy of the several definitions which degrade man below the level of beasts. Despite the multiplication of such definitions in *Gulliver's Travels*, the work itself makes the definition of man problematic.

"I have got materials towards a treatise proving the falsity of that definition *animal rationale*, and to show it should be only *rationis capax*." Thus Swift's own definition, written just after he had finished the *Travels*, in the famous letter to Pope. The treatise unmistakably makes its point: man is certainly not *animal rationale* in the sense conveyed by the portrayal of the Houyhnhnms. But then not even "Dutch Burgersdyck" (the name Pope gives to a horse, incidentally, in *Dunciad* 4) would have supposed he is. Swift is attacking the persistent fallacy which holds that because man is a rational animal, his "real essence," to use Locke's terminology, is to be found in the quality differentiating him from other animals: the fallacy that says, man *is*, essentially, that identifying quality—the fallacy demonstrated by Westminster's Dr. Busby (again in *Dunciad* 4):

> Since man from beast by words is known,
> Words are man's province, words we teach alone.

Instead, Swift maintains, man is an animal possessed of the faculty of reason; he is *rationis capax*—capable of rational behavior (as with the king of Brobdingnag or Don Pedro), but also capable of using reason for the most vicious ends. The probability is overwhelming, Swift knew, that man will use it in the latter way. Swift's

conviction derives from another element in his definition:
the belief, given by his religion, confirmed by his experience, testified to by the whole body of his work, that man
has a corrupt nature. Reason is a noble faculty in itself,
but exercised in the service of a corrupt will it produces
the most disastrous consequences. We are taught "by
the tritest maxim in the world," wrote Swift in the
Apology to *A Tale of a Tub*, "that Religion being the
best of things, its corruptions are likely to be the worst."
The same principle applies to reason, as Gulliver's
Houyhnhnm master warned: "he dreaded lest the corruption of that faculty might be worse than brutality itself."
Corruptio optimi pessima—no theme is more persistent in
Swift's career; it derives its peculiar force from his conviction
that man—*rationis capax*—is a fallen and corrupt creature.

Intimations appear in his work, however (as in Gulliver's experience of the past in Glubbdubdrib), that by
some dispensation a few men may achieve a qualified
virtue, a few societies may attain some measure of
grandeur and felicity.[6] These are objects of wonder,
running counter, as they do, to a law of life based on
degeneration; victories over the corruption of the world
are bound to be rare, precarious, and shortlived. Lilliput
stands as a paradigm case: despite its ideal institutions,
the nation has become infamously corrupt because of "the
degenerate nature of man."[7]

6. Writing of the remarkable piety of early Christians (in "Concerning that Universal Hatred, Which Prevails Against the
Clergy"), Swift once admitted that a long time ago monks lived
austere and virtuous lives "in caves and cells, in desert places.
But when public edifices were erected and endowed, they began
gradually to degenerate into idleness, ignorance, avarice, ambition,
and luxury, after the usual fate of all human institutions."

7. One or two comments in *Gulliver's Travels* tend to qualify
Swift's usual insistence on the theme of man's degeneration.
Gulliver's criticism of the Brobdingnagian moralist (the author

Swift's definition of man measures the degree to which the moral utopia of Houyhnhnmland is available as a model to human beings, in the sense that More's Utopia is available. To be sure, Houyhnhnmland has a good many features in common with other utopian communities. The Houyhnhnms have fairly standard utopian ideas about property, for example—all creatures, they feel, are entitled to their share in the produce of the earth. They have as keen an interest in eugenics as have the citizens of the *Republic* or of Campanella's *City of the Sun*: the Solarians mate large beautiful women with large aggressive men, lean women with fat men, and so on; the Houyhnhnms mate, within a rigidly limited color range, rugged females with comely males, so as to produce the most valued racial characteristics. They practice strict monogamy and strict birth control. When any family has more than the requisite number of children, it follows the custom of More's Utopians and passes the excess onto a family deficient in progeny. In these respects and in others Houyhnhnmland resembles the best-known ideal communities—above all, of course, in the fact that it is a "good place." It is precisely the special character of its goodness, however, that sets Houyhnhnmland markedly apart from other lands of its kind.

Most utopias recognize the power of evil in man, even when they do not accept a doctrine of his total corruption.

---

of the "little old treatise") who repines at the degeneration of nature and the "small abortive births" of the present is probably to be taken straightforwardly; Swift, that is, makes the moralist (and to some degree the theme) seem silly. Again, Gulliver brags that had he been born a *struldbrugg*, the example of his and his companions' lives "would probably prevent that continual degeneracy of human nature so justly complained of in all ages." Anything "justly complained of in all ages" in Gulliver's mouth is suspect; the theme of degeneracy is not exempt.

Robert Burton, working out the "Utopia of mine own"
in the *Anatomy of Melancholy*, writes: "If it were possible,
I would have such priests as should imitate Christ, charit-
able lawyers as should love their neighbors as themselves, temperate and modest physicians. . . ." But, says
Burton, "we converse here with men, not with gods"
and proceeds to elaborate a set of sternly repressive
regulations.[8] Although many utopias are less rigid than
Burton's, their method is the same: in order to achieve
the good life, they rely upon education, upon carefully
worked out laws strictly enforced, upon institutions
conceived in such a way as to encourage man's
potentialities for good and to mitigate his potentialities
for evil. Nearly always, that is, a parameter in the problem
of designing a utopia is the knowledge that man can be
very wicked indeed. The Houyhnhnms, who cannot
conceive of what is evil in a rational creature, who find it
unnecessary to struggle to achieve virtue, have not the
human curse to cope with. Their utopia is *given*, like the
Golden Age; it is not *created* in terms applicable to the
human condition. To be sure, there is a principle of corruption in Houyhnhnmland—the Yahoos are the very
embodiment of corruption—but they embody the corruption completely. The Yahoos cannot taint the Houyhnhnms, to whom they are neither threat nor temptation.
Without an internal source of degeneration, and with the
assumption that no more Englishmen violate their seclu-
sion, the utopia of the Houyhnhnms will presumably
endure forever. The distance between this ideal and the
reality of man as Swift knew him is quite unbridgeable.

8. *Anatomy of Melancholy*, pp. 56–63. The epigraph to Mary
McCarthy's *The Oasis* (New York: Random House, 1949), a
satirical fiction about a utopian colony, is a passage from Rousseau's
Confessions: "In fact, it must be confessed that, both in this world
and the next, the wicked are always a source of considerable
embarrassment."

Gulliver tries, and ends up, back in England, talking to horses.

Perhaps it was from the stable that Gulliver wrote to Captain Sympson, complaining of those readers of his travels who hinted that "the Houyhnhnms and Yahoos have no more existence than the inhabitants of Utopia." In a sense they have even less existence: the Houyhnhnms (if not the Yahoos) are a good deal more remote from man and his possibilities than are the people of More's imaginary land—more remote even than inhabitants of the Republic, the only commonwealth, Socrates warned, in whose politics the enlightened man can ever take part. But the Houyhnhnms have no politics. Both Raphael Hythloday and Gulliver long to live in the lands they have discovered. By the ironic twist at the end of *Utopia* More indicates that, for his voyager, he would approve—and Peter Giles thinks that Hythloday may be on his way back to the place he loves. Utopia is a long way from Houyhnhnmland, however; and Swift, whose moral realism Ricardo Quintana celebrated years ago, had little use for Gulliver's aspirations. The purity of the horses is preternatural—ideal in some sense, surely, but not as a model for man. Despite his own utopian predispositions, Swift was not of the Houyhnhnm party; he was not a designer of ideal societies which require the wholesale remaking of man. As a satirist willing to bring his own *folie raisonnante* to the test of his own ridicule, he *could not* be that kind of utopian. In a way, Swift was a Popperian before Professor Popper, shunning the grandiose social blueprint, cutting away instead at gross and corrigible evils; hence the predominance of satire in his most utopian work. No, Swift was not of the Houyhnhnm party: a utopian without illusions, he hoped that man could live in Brobdingnag.

4

Hawthorne & Utopia

The Blithedale Romance

Hawthorne's *Blithedale Romance* is, of course, not a utopia in any strict sense; it does not belong to the genre at the center of which are works like More's *Utopia*, Bellamy's *Looking Backward*, Morris's *News from Nowhere*. On the other hand, *The Blithedale Romance* is related in the most interesting way to actual utopian experiments in history—Brook Farm, specifically—and it dramatizes certain problematic questions about utopia that have had major consequence for the twentieth century. Thus the relationship of *Blithedale* to the generic problems with which we are concerned has seemed to me significant enough to justify a close look at Hawthorne's romance.

This essay was first published in *Hawthorne Centenary Essays*, edited by Roy Harvey Pearce (© 1964 by the Ohio State University Press; all rights reserved), and is reprinted by permission.

Miles Coverdale projects the romance of Blithedale into the future one summer day, as he and Hollingsworth lift stones into place to repair a wall. In a century or two, he says to his silent companion, Zenobia, Priscilla, Hollingsworth, and he will be mythic characters; legends will have grown up about them, and they will figure heroically in an epic poem. But to Hollingsworth feckless speculations like these are infuriating; the utopian project at Blithedale is, in his view, a wretched, insubstantial scheme, impossible of realization and worthless if possible. "It has given you a theme for poetry," he growls at Coverdale. "Let that content you."

It is a question whether Hawthorne's experience at Brook Farm brought him more, although he boasted, according to Emerson, of having lived in the utopian community during its heroic age. He was there, on his own explanation, to find a way of supporting a wife, but he was there against the grain. A shy, solitary man, Hawthorne was always cool to reform movements, always skeptical of the possibility of progress. Still, impelled by whatever unaccountable enthusiasm, he left Boston for Brook Farm in April 1841 and arrived (like his fictional counterpart at Blithedale) in a snowstorm: "Here I am in a polar Paradise!" he wrote to his fiancée Sophia Peabody. He labored manfully, though with rapidly diminishing enthusiasm, in the "gold-mine"— that is, the manure pile—and in the fields; and, predictably, he became disaffected. The proposed union between intellectual and manual labor turned out to be less natural than had been hoped. Brook Farm proved, said Elizabeth Peabody, Sophia's bluestocking sister, that "gentlemen, if they will work as many hours as boors, will succeed even better in cultivating a farm." Hawthorne was more interested in the harsher lesson on the other side of the coin: "a man's soul may be buried and perish under a dungheap, or in a furrow of the field, just as well as in a pile of money." Hawthorne left Brook Farm before the end of the year; what it was he sought there he had not found. But he had been given a theme for poetry.

True, Hawthorne denied it, claiming that he had from Brook Farm not a theme but a theater where the creatures of his imagination could play out their "phantasmagorical antics." It was no part of his purpose, he said, to deal in his fiction with his former associates of the socialist community or to make any judgment with respect to socialism itself. Brook Farm offered itself as the setting for his romance because it was the closest analogue he could find to the poetic and fairy precincts, shadowed and obscure, so abundantly available to Old World romancers, so lamentably lacking in the sunshine of America. He chose Brook Farm because in a special sense it was unreal. His own experience there had been unreal even at the time he was living it. "It already looks like a dream behind me," he writes to Sophia Peabody during a fortnight's vacation from the rigors of farm work. His life at Brook Farm is, he says, an "unnatural . . . and therefore an unreal one." Ten years later the experience has been transmuted into the most romantic episode of his career: "essentially a day-dream, and yet a fact—and thus offering an available foothold between fiction and reality." In short, an American setting for romance.

Critics argue that the American genius for fiction has expressed itself most characteristically and most brilliantly in the romance, with its infusion of the mysterious, rather than in the novel proper, with its sturdy grounding in the actual, the solid, the real. Given *Moby Dick* and *The Scarlet Letter*, we would be churlish to complain. Many readers of *The Blithedale Romance* have wished, however, that in this instance the allurements of the mysterious had given way in Hawthorne's mind to a concern for the actual; we would gladly trade veiled ladies and handsome villains with false teeth and snake-headed canes for a Flemish portrait of Brook Farm. Admittedly, the book has aroused a good deal of speculation about whether it is in fact a *roman à clef*, and some members of Brook Farm felt that Hawthorne's portrayal had done them injustice; but in truth so little of the actuality of Brook Farm appears in the work that, as Henry James said, the complaining brethren had more reason to feel slighted than misrepresented.

Hawthorne's refusal as an artist to confront the political and sociological issues posed by Brook Farm is one of a series of evasions that make *The Blithedale Romance* tantalizing, slippery, finally unsatisfactory as a work of art. His choice of the setting at Brook Farm necessarily entailed legitimate expectations from readers. This is a matter of history and fact, not of literary device. Brook Farm was famous even in its failure; interest was high in the social theory by which it had operated and in the great personalities who had been attracted to it. When *The Blithedale Romance* appeared (five years after the final break-up of the Association), many people concluded immediately that Zenobia's character was modelled upon that of Margaret Fuller, whose close association with Brook Farm (although she was not a member) was widely known. Miss Fuller's tragic death—like Zenobia's, by drowning—two years before *Blithedale's* publication was a significant link in the identification and revived interest in Brook Farm itself. Most important, Hawthorne had been there—a witness and participant in an episode that was real in American history, if not in his own imagination. Given these special circumstances, the setting of his book created its own demands; it cried out for detailed, novelistic treatment: for description and solidity of specification and judgment as the novelist appropriately renders these. But Hawthorne evaded such claims by his choice of form, which precluded, he said, "the actual events of real lives," as well as a moral or political judgment of socialism. He wanted it both ways at once—the romance of Brook Farm without the commitment that evaluation would have entailed. The evasion provoked some readers to indignation. Would he have refused judgment similarly if his setting had been a picturesque slave plantation? demanded George Eliot.[1]

Despite Hawthorne's disclaimers, judgment of the utopian experiment at Blithedale does of course emanate from the book—not, however, the kind of judgment that comes from intense scrutiny of the workings of the community: its hopes, tensions, follies, achievements, failures. We see almost nothing of this. Judgment comes instead from scattered comments, mostly unfavorable, of two or three principal characters and from the pervading tone of the work, which is imparted by the narrator, by Miles Coverdale, minor poet, *voyeur extraordinaire*, assiduous parrot of Hawthorne's journals, dubious spokesman for his creator. Coverdale's relations with Blithedale are most complex. One is never sure, for example, why he made the initial plunge: why he puffed out the final whiff of cigar smoke and left his bachelor rooms in Boston —the fire burning in the grate, the closet stocked with champagne and claret—to sally out, as he puts it, "into the heart of the pitiless snowstorm, in quest of a better life." The gesture is generous, idealistic, self-revealing, and Coverdale hastens to clothe himself in irony. He speaks with mock grandiloquence of his own "heroism," of "the mighty hearts" of his companions and himself, which

1. Review article in *Westminster Review* 58 (1852):318–21. For identification of authorship, see James D. Rust, "George Eliot on *The Blithedale Romance*," *Boston Public Library Quarterly* 7 (1955):207–15.

barely had throbbing room in the narrow streets of Boston, of their task: "the reformation of the world." The mannered hyperbole belittles both the speaker and the enterprise on which he is launched. It is a consistent tone.

From the beginning Miles Coverdale has doubts about the legitimacy of the Blithedale venture. His first meeting with Zenobia, that magnificent woman, throws everything else out of focus: her mere presence at Blithedale, her insistent reality, caused the Arcadian enterprise to seem a sham. Occasionally Coverdale takes a positive stance, as in his fine climactic scene with Hollingsworth where he speaks fervently of "this fair system of our new life, which has been planned so deeply, and is now beginning to flourish so hopefully around us. How beautiful it is, and, as far as we can yet see, how practicable!" But more characteristically Coverdale laughs aloud in mocking recognition of the ridiculousness of their utopian scheme. Like Hawthorne with Brook Farm, Coverdale can doubt the reality of the whole experience. A few days away from the farm and it all comes to seem "dream work and enchantment" to him. The lofty aims and fine assurances of the first few days have evaporated; what remains in his mind is the deadening reality of hard work.

In his most ambitious moments of assessment, years after the experience, Coverdale makes explicit the duality of his feeling toward Blithedale. The enterprise was folly, he muses, but admirable folly. It was a vision, impossible of achievement but worthy to be followed. It was generous, but fully as absurd as generous. Coverdale had toyed with utopia and seen it fail; and like a middle-aged American of the 1960s, looking back on a rash plunge into political experience in the thirties, he is proud that he once had the idealism to be misled.

Coverdale's ambivalence toward Blithedale is a favorable judgment compared to other evaluations. Hollingsworth is contemptuous of the project from the beginning, seeing it as a miserably frivolous thing compared to his own scheme for reforming criminals. Zenobia at first takes something of Coverdale's tone as she plays with self-conscious irony on the notion that they are reconstituting Paradise. But at the end, after her fortune is presumed gone and Hollingsworth has thrust her aside for Priscilla, her condemnation is bitter: "I am weary of this place, and sick to death of playing at philanthropy and progress. Of all varieties of mock-life, we have surely blundered into the very emptiest mockery, in our effort to establish the one true system." Even Westervelt adds his variation on the theme as he ridicules the inhabitants of this latter-day Forest of Arden.

Thus every major character in the book (except Priscilla) contributes to the notion that life at Blithedale is mock-life, artificial, insubstantial. As in the masquerade scene, everything is "put on" for the pastoral occasion; and the pastoral is the most studiedly artificial of genres. Miles Coverdale, who confesses to having a decided tendency toward the actual, finds himself getting so far out of reckoning with the real that he has to leave Blithedale to get his moorings once more. For reality Coverdale goes to Boston.

An odd twist shows here. The very quality of life which made Brook Farm available to Hawthorne as the setting for his romance constitutes, in the mouths of his characters, a criticism of the socialist experiment at Blithedale. This critique may be summed up by citing Coverdale's harsh comment on the manner Zenobia chose for her death: her drowning had "some tint of the Arcadian affectation that had been visible enough in all our lives, for a few months past."

Here, singly and in sum, is judgment in plenty on Blithedale; and no voice is raised in opposition. Is it

Hawthorne's judgment? Given the operative conventions of fiction, of course it is not. Furthermore, many of the negative criticisms have the most dubious bearing on the utopian experiment. Any remark of Westervelt, for example, can be immediately dismissed because he is the devil, or a very near relative. Hollingsworth is a monomaniac, incapable of seeing beyond his own incredible scheme for criminal rehabilitation; his opinions of Blithedale lack cogency in proportion as he lacks balance. Zenobia's denunciation of the "mock-life" of Blithedale tells heavily against the community, but as criticism it is not earned by the experience depicted in the book. Zenobia is sick to death, not of the socialist experiment, but of the perversity of a New England blacksmith who could choose the debile and childlike Priscilla over her own opulent self. Psychologically plausible as it is, Zenobia's outburst reveals far more of her own sickness than any of Blithedale's. "Take the moral of Zenobia's history," writes George Eliot, "and you will find that Socialism is apparently made responsible for consequences which it utterly condemned." George Eliot overstates, but in a way that the economy of the book abets.

Miles Coverdale is the only character in the romance whose judgment of Blithedale bears directly and with relevance on the kind of experience Hawthorne had lived at Brook Farm. Coverdale is ambivalent, as we have seen, proud at one moment to be on the point of progress as it thrusts out into chaos, shrewdly skeptical the next as (like Friedrich Engels) he reflects on the anomalous position of a utopian community forced to compete for livelihood with the world it has rejected. This is practical criticism, however, not moral judgment. A condition of moral judgment—if it is to carry weight—is that we have full confidence in the judge: in his character and sensitivity as well as his wisdom, in his human sympathy.

Coverdale is not a man to inspire such confidence. True, his frank characterization of himself allows his charm and intelligence to come through; and his very frankness in revealing his own failures of character predisposes us to sympathy toward him. This is one of a number of seductive consequences following upon our being exposed to a sustained "inside view" narrative. But sympathy falters when Coverdale tells us of the "cold tendency" which makes him pry into other people's passions—a tendency, he says, that has helped unhumanize his heart. He shows us himself in a series of scenes as a compulsive Peeping Tom (he even dreams of peeping); we see him being sadistically cruel to Priscilla, malevolent to Zenobia, bitterly revengeful toward Hollingsworth. What are we to make of a man who, looking back over the avowed emptiness of his life, searches his mind for a cause worth dying for and finds one, in these terms: "If Kossuth . . . would pitch the battlefield of Hungarian rights within an easy ride of my abode, and choose a mild, sunny morning, after breakfast, for the conflict, Miles Coverdale would gladly be his man, for one brave rush upon the levelled bayonets. Further than that, I should be loath to pledge myself." Somewhere Coverdale refers to the "customary levity" of his speech; the phrase characterizes precisely the tone of his moral life. He is not one—Hawthorne will not let him be one—whose judgment of the utopian experiment at Blithedale can command assent.

Thus, although there are many judgments of Blithedale in the book, none of them—singly or in combination—can be said to represent Hawthorne's own final and reliable judgment; in this sense his disclaimer in the preface is justified. One must feel that this is a major weakness of the work—the weakness that Henry James was touching upon, I think, when, with his eye upon opportunities lost, he complained that Hawthorne was not a satirist. "There is no satire whatever in the *Romance*," he lamented; "the quality is almost conspicuous by its absence."[2] This is not entirely accurate. Zenobia sometimes functions as a satirist; she spins a fine satirical fantasy on Coverdale turned country bumpkin, for example—the fantasy a sharp critique of the sentimentality of Blithedale values. Westervelt, that implausible villain, draws a deft satirical portrait of Hollingsworth and is so overcome with delight at his accomplishment that he bursts into metallic laughter, disclosing thereby the brilliant sham of his dental arrangements. Even Miles Coverdale demonstrates an occasional feeling for the tone of satire, as when he decides (mistakenly) that Hollingsworth is, after all, a philanthropic man—"not that steel engine of the devil's contrivance, a philanthropist!" All this is quite incidental though and does not affect the validity of James's point. What is wanted at the heart of the book is the stringency of the satiric view.

The difficulty is bound up in the conception of Miles Coverdale, a narrator whose self-protecting irony enables him to avoid taking a rigorous stand on anything. The most common rhetorical pattern in Coverdale's musings throughout the book consists in a statement of judgment or conclusion—this followed immediately by a new sentence beginning with "But . . .," which retracts or qualifies or blurs what has just been stated. Coverdale is the classically uncommitted man; he could hardly have been a satirist any more than he could have been a single-minded utopian.

The Blithedale Romance puts a critical problem very like that encountered in More's *Utopia* and in *Gulliver's Travels*: what is the relation between the author of the

2. *Hawthorne* (London: Macmillan and Company, 1879), p. 88; cf. p. 137.

work and the character the author created to tell of utopia? If we look at *The Blithedale Romance* with a post-Jamesian eye, it is possible to think of Miles Coverdale as an "unreliable narrator," in Wayne Booth's terms, with Hawthorne standing in a critically ironic relation to him. Hawthorne, after all, is the one who makes Coverdale display himself as a deplorably inadequate human being. "I have made but a poor and dim figure in my own narrative," Coverdale writes at the end. At times, Hawthorne seems to be laughing at his alter ego. In the grotesque voyeur scene in Boston, for example, Coverdale has been caught out by Westervelt and Zenobia as he peeps into their window across the street. Zenobia, hurling a glance of scorn, drops a window curtain between them. The speed with which Coverdale rationalizes his outrageous behavior can be nothing short of comic: "I had a keen, revengeful sense of the insult inflicted by Zenobia's scornful recognition, and more particularly by her letting down the curtain; as if such were the proper barrier to be interposed between a character like hers and a perceptive faculty like mine." The play on words here is amusing and pointed (Coverdale is consistently proud of his delicate intuitions but relies overmuch on his excellent eyesight); it reinforces our momentary sense that Hawthorne may be mocking his narrator, and for a moment we feel that we are in a work like Mary McCarthy's *Oasis*, where Coverdale would be perfectly at home.

When we look for further evidence of this kind, however, evidence developed at all systematically, we of course do not find it. So little ironic remove is there between Hawthorne and Coverdale that we are forced to think of the play on "perceptive faculty" as either unintentional or as an isolated, and therefore incoherent, flash of wit. If Hawthorne deliberately created Coverdale as an unreliable narrator (and in some sense he unquestionably did so create him), he provided almost no clues by which the reader could redress the unreliability.[3] He is no more a satirist with respect to Coverdale than Coverdale is a satirist with respect to the utopia he left. Neither Blithedale nor the man who tells of Blithedale is finally *placed* in the moral (which is to say, the fictive) structure of the book. This is a limitation sanctioned only superficially by the form Hawthorne chose; the true limitation, we must feel, is in the romancer, not the romance.

A radical incoherence exists at the heart of *The Blithedale Romance*: the Veiled Lady-Fauntleroy-Westervelt business has no meaningful relation with the thematic interests of the work, nor do these interests reveal themselves in notable harmony. It occurs to me that the harmony was available, implicit in the experience described, but that Hawthorne failed finally to achieve it because, like Coverdale, he remained a witness and refused the role of judge. Or, if this is overstated, at least Hawthorne refused to push his judgment to a point at which he would have been able to unify the ideological materials with which he worked.

Of course certain morals are drawn in the clearest terms. Zenobia is a figure straight out of homiletic literature, out of Juvenal, say, or *The Vanity of Human Wishes*. All that makes her the superb woman she is— her vitality, her intelligence, her radiant sexuality—all that sets her apart as a figure of heroic drama, conspires to her ruin. She is what she is because she lives "out of

3. The alternative is to conclude with Frederick C. Crews, "A New Reading of *The Blithedale Romance*," *American Literature* 29 (May 1957): 147–70, that the book is constructed with the fiendish ingenuity of a Nabokov novel. The interpretation, interesting as it is, does not hold up.

the beaten track"; and it is this, she says, drawing her own bitter moral, that pulls the universe down upon her.

Hollingsworth's career is even more clearly an exemplum; the analysis of his character is relentless as we are made to see into what makes this gifted man move, as we watch him, impelled by noble motives, become dehumanized under the pressure of the *idée fixe* that rules him. Men like Hollingsworth, remarks Coverdale, are not motivated so much as *incorporated* by their single principle. "And the higher and purer the original object, and the more unselfishly it may have been taken up, the slighter is the probability that they can be led to recognize the process by which godlike benevolence has been debased into all-devouring egotism." As self-consecrated high priests, they will sacrifice whatever is most precious before their idol, in whose features they see only benignity and love. Hollingsworth's own soul is doomed to be corrupted, Coverdale sees, by the overweening purpose which had grown out of what was noblest in him. The shape of the corruption is delineated by Zenobia as at the end she sees the man she has loved for what he is. "Are you a man? No; but a monster! A cold, heartless, self-beginning and self-ending piece of mechanism!" Hawthorne's theme is as old as Aristotle—the same one we saw in Swift: *corruptio optimi pessima.*

Blithedale itself might have been encompassed by the same moral referents had Hawthorne chosen to show us, in concrete terms, the community recapitulating in large the progress of its most powerful member. The theme is broached, as a matter of fact, although in fairly abstract terms. We know that the community of Blithedale originates out of the most generous motives, that it is dedicated to the loftiest aims, and that it falls victim to corruption generated out of its own virtues. Blithedale failed, and deserved to fail, says Coverdale in retrospect, because it lapsed into Fourierism. (Three years after Hawthorne left Brook Farm the members announced officially that they gave unqualified assent to the principles of Fourier and proposed to organize themselves into a "perfect Phalanx," with, presumably, the total systematization of life in the interests of happiness that implied.) Coverdale's remark recalls an earlier scene. During his convalescence at Blithedale he read widely in Fourier, ploughing through the eccentric volumes because he recognized an analogy between Fourier's system and their own, opposed as their respective principles might be. Coverdale explains parts of Fourier's system to Hollingsworth and translates some of the more egregious passages for his benefit. They take particular delight in Fourier's famous prophecy that in the fullness of progress the ocean shall be transformed into lemonade. Both men are contemptuous of Fourier's principles and his grandiose plans: he has, says Coverdale, "searched out and discovered the whole counsel of the Almighty, in respect to mankind, past, present, and for exactly seventy thousand years to come by the mere force of his individual intellect!" Hollingsworth is outraged that Fourier should choose man's selfishness as the motive force for his system. "To seize upon and foster whatever vile, petty, sordid, filthy, bestial and abominable corruptions have cankered into our nature, to be the efficient instruments of his infernal regeneration!" The devil himself could contrive no worse. "And his consummated Paradise, as he pictures it, would be worthy of the agency which he counts upon for establishing it."

How remarkable Hawthorne's prescience is!—his sensitivity to the signals that issues of the future send out before them. Here we have two men, members of a utopian community, discussing the corruption of the utopian principle, seeing that in the absolutism of Fourier's vision, however humane and nonrestrictive it may seem,

lies the potentiality of a utopian hell. Coverdale's reference
to the awful truth in *Pilgrim's Progress*—"from the very
gate of heaven there is a by-way to the pit"—is made with
Hollingsworth in mind; but its application in this context
is exact. Hawthorne is on the verge of one of the twentieth century's most compulsive themes, the fear of utopia.
He touches on issues which were to be worked out fully
by Dostoevski (in *The Devils* and *The Brothers Karamazov*),
Zamyatin, Huxley, Neil Gunn (in the neglected *Green
Isle of the Great Deep*)—issues which are central to the
crisis in ideology of our day. *Corruptio optimi pessima*
sums it up well enough.

Remarkable as Hawthorne's insight is, however, we
must not claim for him too much. The discussion of
utopianism is brief and abstract. In only the most casual way
is it made to bear on Blithedale: the community fell into
Fourierism, says Coverdale years after the event, and de-
servedly failed. We are not allowed to *see* that failure: how it
was and what it meant. Coverdale's remark has a factual
bearing only; it is not the statement of a novelist.[4]

In his essay on *The Blithedale Romance* Irving Howe
speaks of the temptation to write about the book it might
have been rather than the book it is.[5] I am conscious of
having succumbed to that temptation—an arrogant
procedure perhaps, but not entirely gratuitous. Hawthorne chose to write a romance, which in this instance
entailed "phantasmagoric antics," "Sybilline attributes,"

4. *The Blithedale Romance* is a mine of rich themes that Hawthorne
opens but does not work out. The relationship of Zenobia to
Priscilla never comes clear, but it implies everything James was to
develop fully in the Chancellor-Tarrant relation in *The Bostonians*.
See Marius Bewley, *The Complex Fate* (London: Chatto & Windus,
1952), p. 19.

5. "Hawthorne—Pastoral and Politics," *New Republic* (5 Sep-
tember 1955), p. 19; the essay is included in Howe's *Politics and the
Novel* (New York: Horizon Press, 1957).

satanic stigmata. Such materials, with their vague intimations of allegorical significance, could not have been of great interest even to a receptive nineteenth-century audience; they are of no possible interest today. Hawthorne also chose his setting, which for historical reasons was bound to be interesting and to generate its own demands; perhaps inadvertently he found himself in the dilemma of the historical novelist, where "background" takes on independent life and moves to the fore, disrupting the normal relation of figure to ground. In any event, his setting could be successfully rendered only in proportion as he was willing to introduce "reality" into its presentation—the kind of reality that Miles Coverdale discovers in a picture in a Boston saloon and rejects.

Coverdale, we recall, once toyed with the fancy that he might figure as a hero in the future epic poem celebrating Blithedale. A poet himself, it would never have occurred to him that he might write that poem. Zenobia, who sees the whole affair as a tragedy, accuses him of trivializing it, of turning it into a ballad. When she suggests a moral for his poem, he wants to soften it. The ballad, one fears, will be sentimental.

Hawthorne's situation once again runs parallel to that of the poet he created. He was by no means the man by conviction or temperament to write the epic of Brook Farm. Nor was he prepared to write a novel (to say nothing of a satirical novel) grounded in range and depth in his own experience of the attempt to establish a utopia; to do this would have required that he commit himself, that he *judge* what he had lived in a way that he was unwilling to undertake. His choice of romance as the form to incorporate his material gave him at least superficial justification for evading these issues. The aesthetic choice was at the same time a moral choice. It is impossible not to wish that he had chosen differently.

❦ 5 ❧

The Fear
of
Utopia

"'Utopia,'" a writer in *Encounter* announced a few years ago, "has become a bad word." As if to prove his point, the bad word was worked hard when in the summer of 1961 the Soviet Union published a statement of the new program by which it proposed to bring communism to the Russian people within this generation. Scores of Western writers used the term "utopian" to belabor Mr. Khrushchev's vision, not only as something remote and unattainable—*Le Monde*'s story carried the sardonic headline "La Promesse de l'age d'or"—but as something evil. Utopia, as we have seen, has always in some sense been related to satire, and Marx used the word as a bludgeon; but the generally unpleasant associations investing the term today are relatively new. Although one would need a very large computer to plot in detail the course of "utopia's" fall from grace, the evidence of literature is adequate to provide an outline of the descent.

By and large usage has been faithful to Thomas More's punning coinage: the play on the Greek *ou topos*: no place, and *eu topos*: good place. The two senses—the one associated with escape into the timeless fantasies of the imagination, the other with the effort to construct models of the ideal society, whether in fiction or otherwise—are inextricably bound up in our use of the term today. But if More coined the word, he was by no means the first to give form to man's longing for a good society. Behind utopia lies the myth of the Golden Age. We might say that the technological abundance of Edward Bellamy's *Looking Backward* is an analogue of the rivers of wine in the Land of Cockaigne.

The difference of course is that the rivers of wine represent longing; the free goods in the warehouses of Bellamy's Boston—or of the Moscow of 1990—represent possibility. By the nineteenth century Western man's fantastically successful command over Nature by means of science and his faith in the inevitability of progress made it seem that utopia—the good society, the good life for man— was a necessary consequence of present historical processes. The presses groaned under the weight of projects. "We were all a little mad that winter," wrote Emerson, recalling the year 1840. "Not a man of us that did not have a plan for some new Utopia in his pocket." Despite harrowing anxieties which underlay much of the speculation, life seemed to move inexorably toward a new Golden Age.

Consider H. G. Wells. After the cosmic gloom of some of the early romances, he issued a flood of utopian speculations founded on the assumption shared by leaders of the Soviet Union and most social scientists: by analyzing scientifically the processes of the present, man can bring the conditions of the future within the range of his knowledge, so that he can control the form of that future. The Shape of Things to Come can be known, and altered for the better. Wells's optimism burgeoned out of control, and history, in revenge, has made him seem a pathetic figure. His last book, written in 1945, was called *Mind at the End of Its Tether*. Here in a sad little postscript to his life he commits the bulk of his work to the laboratory sink: "The attempt to trace a pattern of any sort is absolutely futile," he writes. It is a bitter irony and a measure of the appalling distance that separates Wells's world from our own that his despairing recognition of futility offers the only hope available to a good many Western intellectuals today. If we could see the shape of things to come, say some existentialists, we would cut our throats. Only our historical ignorance prevents total despair; because the future is impenetrable, writes Gabriel Marcel, we can still place a wager on it and so keep going.

As for utopia, it is a bad word. The simplest historical comparison is devastating in its clarity and implication. For John Milton, utopia was a "... grave and noble invention which the ... sublimest wits in sundry ages, *Plato* ... and our two famous countreymen [Thomas More and Francis Bacon], chose, I may not say as a field, but as a mighty Continent wherein to display the largenesse of their spirits by teaching this our world better and exacter things, then were yet known, or us'd ...."[1] Two hundred and fifty years later Anatole France could write: "Without the utopians of other times, men would still live in caves, miserable and naked; ... utopia is the principle of all progress, and the essay into a better world." But today, instead of fictional renderings

1. "An Apology," *Works*, ed. F. A. Patterson and others (New York: Columbia University Press, 1931), vol. 3, pt. 1, pp. 294–95.

of these heady statements of confidence, we have Orwell's *1984* and science-fiction visions of the horrors that await us if we survive. Of course the reason for this radical shift is painfully obvious: to have faith in the possibility of utopia, one must believe in progress; but one looks back at our two great wars, our mass bombings, our attempts at genocide—our collective plunge into barbarism; one hears the Geiger counters of the world clicking away—and it is next to impossible for a rational man to believe in progress. To believe in utopia one must believe that through the exercise of their reason men can control and in major ways alter for the better their social environment; but few men outside some of the Communist countries any longer have faith in the power of reason to bring about desired political ends of large magnitude. To believe in utopia one must have faith of a kind that our history has made nearly inaccessible. This is one major form of the crisis of faith under which Western culture reels.[2]

There are, however, China, the Soviet Union, and those Marxists whose allegiance to the vision has remained unshaken by events of the last thirty-five years. A. L. Morton, a historian of utopian fiction, claims that the belief which has lain at the roots of all utopian writing of the past—the belief in the capacity and the splendid future of mankind—has already been vindicated in Russia. Utopia has in fact been realized there—this written in the year 1952, the year before Stalin's death. One man's utopia is another man's—particularly a disillusioned man's—nightmare; and unquestionably the gravest blow to our conviction that, by a sweeping reconstitution of his society, man can create a good world for himself, has

2. For full documentation, see Judith N. Shklar, *After Utopia: The Decline of Political Faith* (Princeton: Princeton University Press, 1957).

come from the experience of the Soviet Union itself. Some sense of the limitless possibilities that experience once held out for a whole generation comes through what André Gide writes after the disillusionment of his stay in Russia: "Who can ever say what the Soviet Union had been for me? Far more than the country of my choice, an example and an inspiration, it represented what I had always dreamed of but no longer dared hope— it was something toward which all my longing was directed—it was a land where I imagined Utopia was in process of becoming reality. . . . I was ready to throw myself with all my heart into the contract, as it were, into which I had entered with the Soviet Union in the name of all suffering mankind. I felt myself so much committed that failure was not to be contemplated."[3]

But Gide himself and Koestler, Richard Wright, Camus, Auden, Spender, and countless others had to contemplate the failure, had to recognize it, had agonizingly to come to terms with it. The god had failed, and the story of his failure is a polygraph of the death of utopian faith in our time. "The tragedy of our generation," says Camus, "is to have seen a false hope."

In a way this record of disillusionment and despair (sketchily suggested here) accounts for the fact that we have almost no utopian literature today. Conceivably this may change. The utopian spirit is once again manifest in certain elements of the generation after Camus—in primitivistic form with the hippies and their cohorts, in militant form among the students. Utopia has its philosophers: Herbert Marcuse (his recent *Essay on Liberation* explicity repudiates the Marxian injunction against utopian speculation), Norman O. Brown, Paul Goodman,

3. In *The God That Failed*, ed. R. H. S. Crossman (New York: Harper, 1949), p. 180.

Norman Mailer, to speak only of the United States. But thus far it remains true that in literature, which so often breaks new paths into possibility for philosophers and politicians to follow, the theme of utopia no longer engages the imagination. Instead, we have utopias in negative—scores of them—which, with their selective distortion of the utopian impulse, satirize, caricature, call into question the idea of utopia itself. Whereas for Bellamy or William Morris present society was the evil to be transcended, and the image of the desirable life was projected into the future, in the negative utopia it is the life of the future, created in response to man's longing for happiness on earth, that is the evil. Utopia is a bad word today not because we despair of being able to achieve it but because we fear it. Utopia itself (in a special sense of the term) has become the enemy.

Nobody has written more cogently on this theme than has Nicolas Berdyaev, whose views were given unexpected currency when Huxley appropriated a passage from *Slavery and Freedom* as the epigraph for *Brave New World*:

> Utopias seem very much more realizable than we had formerly supposed. And now we find ourselves facing a question which is painful in a new kind of way: How to avoid their actual realization? . . . Utopias are realizable. Life moves toward a utopia. And perhaps a new age is beginning, an age in which the intellectuals and the cultivated class will dream of methods of avoiding utopia and of returning to a society that is nonutopian, that is less "perfect" and more free.

Clearly Berdyaev is using the word "utopia" in a very different sense from that of More or Cabet or William Morris; and in his usage is implied a theory about the essential nature of utopia. The theme engaged Berdyaev in book after book. Just before his death, for example, he wrote, movingly, that utopian thought is profoundly inherent in human nature: man, wounded by the evil of the world, inevitably evokes an image of a perfect, harmonious social order where he will be happy. And utopias are realizable; the Bolsheviks are utopians, possessed by the idea of a perfect society. But it is a condition of bringing utopias to pass that they shall be deformed in the process. Man lives in a fragmented world, says Berdyaev, and dreams of an integrated world. This is the essence of utopia: that it is destined to surmount the fragmentation of the world and bring wholeness, *intégralité*. But in that very process human freedom is destroyed. None of the classical utopias have made room for freedom, writes Berdyaev elsewhere: the "aristocratic idealistic communism" of Plato's *Republic*, the prototype of utopias, is, he says, "a thorough-going tyranny, a denial of all freedom and of the value of personality." Similarly, Thomas More, Campanella, Cabet, and others all fail to provide for individual freedom. In sum, for Berdyaev, "utopia is always totalitarian, and totalitarianism, in the conditions of our world, is always utopian."[4]

Berdyaev's passion and his point of view were unquestionably shaped by his bitter experience of the Soviet Union, but I suspect that an even more important influence was operative: behind all his work looms the prophetic figure of Dostoevski, with whom Berdyaev carried on a dialogue across time all his life. Of the greatest importance to him is the profound and enigmatic legend of the Grand Inquisitor in *The Brothers Karamazov*. We recall the scene that Ivan Karamazov conjures up for Alyosha:

4. See *Royaume de l'esprit et royaume de César*, trans. from Russian by Philippe Sabant (Neuchâtel: Delachaux & Niestlé, 1951), pp. 165–66; *The Destiny of Man*, trans. Natalie Duddington (New York: Harper, 1960), pp. 211 ff.; *Dostoevsky*, trans. D. Attwater (New York: Meridian Books, 1957), pp. 191 ff.

the prison cell in sixteenth-century Seville; the appalling monologue that the ninety-year-old Inquisitor hurls at the Prisoner, at Christ, who has returned to earth and been thrust into jail by the Inquisition. The grand Inquisitor accuses Christ of a ghastly failure: He foolishly imposed upon man the intolerable burden of freedom, instead of taking freedom from man and giving him in its place bread and happiness. Christ rejected the three great powers offered by Satan—miracle, mystery, and authority—which alone could have held men in happy subjection. But the Church, says the old Inquisitor, has now corrected Christ's work; it has assumed the three great powers, and men will gladly lay down their freedom in exchange for the reign of peace and happiness that will ensue. Man longs for unity in one unanimous and harmonious ant hill; the Church, out of its love for feeble humanity, wielding the powers that Christ rejected, and ruling according to a noble lie, will be in a position to plan the universal happiness of man. Not quite all will be happy, however; a few, an elite, those who rule and guard the mystery, will suffer; for they will have taken upon themselves the curse of the knowledge of good and evil. But these are a few only; all the rest will be happy in the wholeness of unfreedom.

Here, comments Berdyaev, is utopia, the product of the "euclidian mind" (a phrase Dostoevski himself often used) which is obsessed by the idea of regulating all life by reason and bringing happiness to man, whatever the cost.

The myth of the future utopian state projected by the Grand Inquisitor constitutes a text on which the major negative utopias of our time—Eugene Zamyatin's *We* and Aldous Huxley's *Brave New World*—are imaginative glosses. Zamyatin, an engineer and mathematician, one of Russia's most brilliant young revolutionary writers, composed *We* in 1920 as a satire on forces which were distorting the revolution for which he had struggled.[5] The book first appeared in the United States, translated from the Russian manuscript, in 1924; it was subsequently translated into French and Czech and then back into Russian for European circulation, but it has never been published in the Soviet Union—all this a melancholy preview of the Pasternak-*Dr. Zhivago* affair and the cases of Daniel and Sinyavski, and most recently, Solzhenitsyn.

Zamyatin's novel dramatizes the United State, as it is called, created by the euclidian mind one thousand years from now. Because the book is not well known (it has not been published in England and, in 1967, the British Museum had no copy of the English translation), I shall reproduce a few passages which convey some sense of the issues involved. *We* is D-503's journal; it opens with a quotation from the State newspaper (this is not yesterday's *Pravda*, but the contemporaneity of the situation is so striking that one must struggle to avoid oversimple identifications):

> "In another hundred and twenty days the building of the *Integral* [a gigantic rocket-ship] will be completed. The great historic hour is near, when the first *Integral* will rise into the limitless space of the universe. One thousand years ago your heroic ancestors subjected the whole earth to the power of the United State. A still more glorious task is before you: the integration of the indefinite equation of the Cosmos by the use of the glass, electric, fire-breathing *Integral*. Your mission is to subjugate to the grateful yoke of reason the unknown beings who live on other planets, and who are perhaps still in the primitive state of freedom. If they will not understand that we are bringing them a mathematically faultless happiness, our duty will be to force them to be happy. . . .
> "Long live the United State! Long live the Numbers! Long live the Well-Doer!!!"

5. *We*, trans. Gregory Zilboorg (New York: Dutton, 1959).

After copying this statement from the newspaper, D-503 begins his journal:

> I feel my cheeks burn as I write this. To integrate the colossal, universal equation! To unbend the wild curve, to straighten it out to a tangent—to a straight line! For the United State is a straight line, a great, divine, precise, wise line, the wisest of lines!
>
> I, D-503, the builder of the *Integral*, I am only one of the many mathematicians of the United State. My pen, which is accustomed to figures, is unable to express the march and rhythm of consonance; therefore I shall try to record only the things I see, the things I think, or, to be more exact, the things *we* think.

D-503 calls his book *We* in celebration of the "victory of *all* over one, of the sum over the individual." He has spoken of the mathematically perfect happy life. How does one reduce happiness to mathematics?

> Naturally, having conquered hunger (that is, algebraically speaking, having achieved the total of bodily welfare), the United State directed its attack against the second ruler of the world, against love. At last this element also was conquered, that is, organized and put into a mathematical formula. It is already three hundred years since our great historic *Lex Sexualis* was promulgated: "A Number may obtain a license to use any other Number as a sexual product."
>
> The rest is only a matter of technique. You are carefully examined in the laboratory of the Sexual Department where they find the content of the sexual hormones in your blood, and they accordingly make out for you a Table of sexual days. Then you file an application to enjoy the services of Number so and so, or Numbers so and so. You get for that purpose a checkbook (pink). That is all.
>
> It is clear that under such circumstances there is no reason for envy or jealousy. The denominator of the fraction of happiness is reduced to zero and the whole fraction is converted into a magnificent infiniteness. . . . Hence you

see how the great power of logic purifies everything it
happens to touch. Oh, if only you unknown readers can
conceive this divine power! If you will only learn to follow
it to the end!

Similarly, ethics has been rationalized to a point where its
problems are resolved by adding, subtracting, multiplying,
and dividing. Beauty, we learn, is a function of unfreedom.
The dance of life in the United State is beautiful, D-503
writes in his journal, "because it is an *unfree* movement.
Because the deep meaning of the dance is contained in its
absolute, ecstatic submission, in the ideal *non-freedom.*"
And the end toward which the United State inevitably
tends—the utopia of this utopia—is that in which time and
history are frozen, the state in which nothing happens.

The euclidianism of the United State is graphically
symbolized in its architecture: rectilinear glass buildings,
glistening glass pavements laid out in straight lines,
square harmonies endlessly repeated—a Bauhaus world
gone mad, mirroring the perfect abstractness of an
almost perfect life. Rebels in this brilliantly grotesque
perversion of utopia adopt as their emblem $\sqrt{-1}$, thus
aligning themselves with the struggle of Dostoevski's
Underground Man against the hegemony of two times
two is four.

Let me pull these themes together by quoting one more
passage. D-503's friend, R-13, a poet, describes a poem
he is writing for the *Integral*:

> You see, it is the ancient legend of paradise. . . . That
> legend referred to us of today, did it not? Yes. Only
> think of it, think of it a moment! There were two in paradise
> and the choice was offered to them: happiness without
> freedom, or freedom without happiness. No other choice. . . .
> They, fools that they were, chose freedom. Naturally,
> for centuries afterward they longed for fetters, for the
> fetters of yore. . . . And only we found a way to regain

happiness. . . . No, listen, follow me! The ancient god and
we, side by side at the same table! Yes, we helped god to
defeat the devil definitely and finally. It was he, the devil,
who led people to transgression, to taste pernicious
freedom—he, the cunning serpent. And we came along,
planted a boot on his head, and . . . squash! Done with
him! Paradise again! We returned to the simple-
mindedness and innocence of Adam and Eve. No more
meddling with good and evil and all that; everything is
simple again, heavenly, childishly simple! The Well-Doer,
the Machine, the Cube, the giant Gas Bell, the Guardians—
all these are good. All this is magnificent, beautiful,
noble, lofty, crystalline, pure. For all this preserves our
non-freedom, that is, our happiness . . . Well, in short,
these are the highlights of my little paradise poem.
What do you think of it?

R-13's paradise is that of Ivan Karamazov's Grand
Inquisitor, who appears in *We* as the Well-Doer, a
Socrates-like, bald-headed man before whom D-503 is
summoned at the climax of the work. The Well-Doer
tells D-503 that the "real, algebraic love for humanity
must inevitably be inhuman"; and D-503, together with
nearly all the citizens of the United State, ultimately
finds his true paradise in a lobotomy, an operation that
does away with the atavistic—that is the *human*—urges
that unreasonably have troubled them and marred the
glassy surface of their state.

Zamyatin, a rigorous satirist, a highly gifted stylist—
his style enacting the mechanical rhythms of the future
state—pushes utopia to this conclusion. Given the premises
of the Grand Inquisitor, here are the results. The themes
are there, shockingly clear, rendered as a novelist renders
them—through the felt experience of characters struggling
to become human.

In Aldous Huxley's *Brave New World* Mustapha
Mond, the Controller, is another incarnation of the Grand

Inquisitor, unhappy himself, dedicated to the happiness of the Epsilons, the Deltas, the Betas, and most of the Alphas. Other people's happiness, he acknowledges, is a hard master; he is one who guards the mystery. The state in this New World has taken on the three great powers rejected by Christ: it provides the bread—and soma and the feelies and electro-magnetic golf; and it provides the mystery, the mechanically-induced epiphany of the Solidarity Service ritual. Above all it provides happiness and stability for the truly innocent children of the new paradise—with their institutionalized sex play and their compulsory promiscuity—to whom the knowledge of good and evil is forbidden. The bottles in which they are born enclose them forever.

Again, as in Zamyatin's *We*, the climax of the book comes in a confrontation of the disaffected in utopia with the Grand Inquisitor figure. Mustapha Mond explains to the Savage:

> "The world's stable now. People are happy; they get
> what they want, and they never want what they can't
> get. They're well off; they're safe; they're never ill; they're
> not afraid of death; they're blissfully ignorant of passion
> and old age; they're plagued with no mothers or fathers;
> they've got no wives, or children, or lovers to feel strongly
> about; they're so conditioned that they practically can't
> help behaving as they ought to behave. And if anything
> should go wrong, there's *soma*. Which you go and chuck
> out of the window in the name of liberty, Mr. Savage.
> *Liberty*!" He laughed. "Expecting Deltas to know what
> liberty is!"

The Controller admits the losses entailed by happiness and stability. Great art has been lost, science has been muzzled; truth is a victim and God. But as Mustapha Mond says: "You must make your choice. Our civilization has chosen . . . happiness."

Against this the Savage shouts his plea:

> "I don't want comfort. I want God, I want poetry, I
> want real danger, I want freedom, I want goodness. I
> want sin."
> "In fact," said Mustapha Mond, "you're claiming the
> right to be unhappy."
> "All right then," said the Savage defiantly, "I'm
> claiming the right to be unhappy."
> "Not to mention the right to grow old and ugly and
> impotent; the right to have syphilis and cancer; the right
> to have too little to eat; the right to be lousy; the right to
> live in constant apprehension of what may happen tomorrow;
> the right to catch typhoid; the right to be tortured by
> unspeakable pains of every kind." There was a long
> silence.
> "I claim them all," said the Savage at last.
> Mustapha Mond shrugged his shoulders. "You're
> welcome," he said.

The tone of Huxley's book is sometimes flippant,
sometimes cynical; but he has respected the complexity
of the issues—issues that are a transliteration of those
enunciated with daemonic prescience by Dostoevski.

Orwell's *1984* both fits and does not fit into the pattern.
It does not fit because utopia has traditionally been
concerned with happiness and the good life. There is
nothing of this in *1984*, which is a true *anti*-utopia, a
dystopia. As Philip Rahv has pointed out, the shadow of
the Grand Inquisitor is powerfully present. In the climactic sequence Winston Smith lies on the torture table in
the Ministry of Love. O'Brien, the Inquisitor whom
Winston significantly does not know whether to love or
hate, interrogates him about the Party's relation to
power."Now tell me *why* we cling to power," he asks
Winston. "What is our motive? . . . Go on speak."

> Winston knew in advance what O'Brien would say. That
> the Party did not seek power for its own ends, but only

for the good of the majority. That it sought power because men in the mass were frail cowardly creatures who could not endure liberty or face the truth, and must be ruled over and systematically deceived by others who were stronger than themselves. That the choice for mankind lay between freedom and happiness, and that, for the great bulk of mankind, happiness was better. That the Party was the eternal guardian of the weak, a dedicated sect doing evil that good might come, sacrificing its own happiness to that of others.

Orwell's turn of the screw is deadly: the sentiments of the Grand Inquisitor of Dostoevski's legend come from the lips of a man under torture; and as he proceeds to utter those sentiments in response to O'Brien's question, the new Inquisitor pulls the lever which sends hideous pain coursing through Winston's body. O'Brien contemptuously dismisses the old apologia for totalitarianism. The end of the Party's power, he says, is *not* man's happiness, not that of the stupid utopias of the past—the end of power is *power*—the power to stamp on the human face forever.

Horrifying as the impact of *1984* is, I think it misses by denying the enormous complexity and subtlety of the issues raised by Dostoevski. Totalitarianism of the *1984* brand poses its own gross dangers, of which we cannot help being aware. But the dangers are gross and so identifiable; O'Brien's world, at least at the stage depicted, makes no pretense of being utopian. Whereas the Party of *1984* plans to abolish the orgasm as part of its assault on human happiness, Dostoevski's Grand Inquisitor—and here is the source of his appeal—truly believes in bringing happiness to man, even in forcing him to be happy. He loves man, genuinely, deeply; he has sacrificed —his God, his own happiness—for man's sake. "Know," he says to Christ, "that I too have been in the wilderness,

I too have lived on roots and locusts . . . and I too was striving to stand among thy elect, among the strong and powerful, thirsting to 'make up the number.' But I awakened and would not serve madness. I turned back and joined the ranks of those *who have corrected thy work.* I left the proud and went back to the humble, for the happiness of the humble."

As I read Dostoevski and Zamyatin and Huxley, there sounds at the back of my mind a refrain: Yeats's lines from "The Second Coming":

> *The best lack all conviction, while the worst*
> *Are full of passionate intensity.*

The fear of utopia arises in good part out of a situation which may be characterized by a twist on Yeats's lines— the situation in which the *best* are full of passionate intensity. It is the *best* who, out of their love for suffering humanity and their desire to bring man happiness, may try to impose a euclidian order on the world and find themselves forced into the choice which seems to be ineluctable: the choice between freedom and happiness. Zamyatin and Huxley have dramatized what they take to be the necessary consequence of the choice. Utopia, in their sense, leads to decanted babies and soma or to lobotomy. Thus the two great mock-utopias of the twentieth century contribute their variation on the theme that shadows utopia: *corruptio optimi pessima.*

From Thomas More and William Morris to this: it is a mighty fall. Inevitably "utopia" has become a bad word; but the question whether or not the fall is irretrievable may still be open. In 1946 Aldous Huxley wrote a preface to *Brave New World* in which he again explicitly equates utopia with insanity, with horror, with tyranny; but then an odd thing happens. "If I were now to rewrite the book," says Huxley, "I would offer the Savage a third alternative. Between the utopian and the primitive horns of his dilemma would lie the possibility of sanity— a possibility already actualized, to some extent, in a community of exiles and refugees from the Brave New World, living within the borders of the Reservation." Huxley proceeds to characterize this hypothetical community: its Henry-Georgian economics, its Kropotkinesque politics, its Buddhist religion. The Savage, he says, would be allowed to learn at first hand "about the nature of a society composed of freely co-operating individuals devoted to the pursuit of sanity" before he was "transported to Utopia." At this point the terminological tangle becomes almost hopeless.[6] Clearly Huxley, writing in 1946, could no longer call his hypothetical new society —the third alternative he envisages for the Savage— utopian; the word had been contaminated by history and, in good part, by his own usage. But the thing itself—that for which the word once stood—was still there: the ineradicable human impulse to imagine the terms in which a better life might be led. It survived even the loss of its name.

Fifteen years later Huxley once more reversed himself on "utopia"; he spoke of his last novel, *Island*, as *Brave New World* in reverse and characterized it as a "utopian fantasy," using the term this time in its old and honorific sense. Perhaps this marks the first step in "utopia's" redemption, for if the word is to be redeemed it will

6. For discussion of the tangle, see George Kateb, *Utopia and its Enemies* (New York: Free Press of Glencoe, 1963), esp. pp. 20, 235; Chad Walsh, *From Utopia to Nightmare* (New York: Harper, 1962); Frederik L. Polak, *The Image of the Future*, trans. E. Boulding (Leyden: A. W. Sythoff and New York: Oceana Publications, 1961), 2. 21 ff.; Glenn R. Negley and J. Max Patrick, *Quest for Utopia* (New York: H. Schuman, 1952), pp. 1–22, 574–83.

have to be by someone who, like Huxley, has faced the issues posed by Dostoevski. It will have to be by someone who has followed utopia into the abyss which yawns behind the Grand Inquisitor's vision, and who has then clambered out on the other side. Both he and utopia will have been changed in the process; out of the hard-won understanding there may come new faith in human possibility.

We will never again be able to create imaginative utopias with the easy confidence of the nineteenth century; the terror to which the eschatological vision applied to human affairs has led in our time forecloses that possibility. At the same time we cannot allow the fear of utopia to inhibit completely the "utopian" imagination, which as Berdyaev says, is profoundly part of human nature. Without goals (even if limited goals), without an image of the good life before us, we flounder. If we must in some sense believe in utopia still, we must do so on the condition that we face the Grand Inquisitor in all his power. It is not a confrontation to be lightly dared.

❧ 6 ❧

✒Aesthetics
of
Utopia

The title page identifies Aldous Huxley's *Island* (1962) as a novel. Most reviewers, accepting the designation without question, proceeded to belabor the book accordingly: despite its interesting ideas, one of the worst novels ever written, Frank Kermode decided; and William Barrett, outraged, accused Huxley of abandoning the novelist's task altogether in order to make propaganda. The indignation of other writers who took this line rose in proportion as they resisted the free love and drugs of utopian Pala. Wayne Booth, however, made a start at sorting out the literary issues.[1] Although it calls itself a novel, *Island* actually belongs, he said, to another, non-Leavisonian "great tradition," along with *Gulliver's Travels, Candide, Rasselas,*

1. Kermode, *Partisan Review* 29 (1962):472–73; Barrett, *Atlantic Monthly* 209 (April 1962):155–56; Booth, *Yale Review*, n.s. 51 (1962):630–32.

Erewhon—works which use fictional devices to provoke thought. Booth avowed his interest in *Island*, although he felt unable to pronounce an aesthetic judgment, the criteria for this "nameless and tricky genre" not yet having been worked out. He issued a cordial invitation to critics to do the working.

Northrop Frye and Richard Gerber had already made notable incursions into the field. Gerber's *Utopian Fantasy* (1955), although ostensibly concerned with English utopian fiction from 1900 to 1955, is in fact a wide-ranging and acute study of most of the interesting generic problems. The last third of the book, called "Aesthetic Concretion," deals with precisely the issues that must be clarified if the simple confusions which bedevilled reviewers of *Island* are to be avoided; and if I disagree with Gerber's conclusions, I want to record my admiration for his work.

Gerber sensibly distinguishes between "evolutionary utopias" (fantastic visions of the future based upon a doctrine of evolutionary progress; e.g., Olaf Stapledon's *Last and First Men*) and utopias of social reconstruction. These last he divides into two categories: the scientific, which places emphasis on the material conditions of society (*New Atlantis, Looking Backward*), and the arcadian, which emphasizes personal freedom (*News from Nowhere*, W. H. Hudson's *A Crystal Age*). Each of these modes is characterized by its own philosophical and stylistic problems and possibilities; but according to Gerber, they all share, together with the negative utopia, in a common teleological destiny. "The development towards the novel is part of the logical evolution of the myth-creating utopian imagination, which impatiently proceeds from the general idea to ever greater actualization"; utopian fiction "slowly assumes the shape of a novel." It must of course be a novel of ideas; but this is less a problem than it once was, for, says Gerber, in our day utopia is problematic, full of social and moral conflicts, its characters diversified and individualized, no longer cyphers in a homogeneous mass. Thus, important constituents of the novel are now available to the utopian writer. If utopian fiction can never quite achieve the kind of imaginative reality available to the realistic novelist, still, Gerber insists, the literary success of the utopia will depend upon how closely it approximates that reality.[2]

These observations clearly apply to the negative utopia more readily (although, as we shall see, still imperfectly) than to the old-fashioned, straightforward, nearly extinct depiction of an ideal society; and in fact Gerber selects *Brave New World* and *1984* as the great literary successes of the utopian form. The cards are stacked, however; Gerber sets up his aesthetic criteria in such a way as to preclude the possibility of literary excellence for the positive utopia. This is gratuitously harsh on an honorable, if unnovelistic, mode of fiction.

Utopian society systematically attempts to eliminate social conflict, accident, tragedy—precisely those elements which make for the fictional development Gerber celebrates. Marxists dream of a time when the state shall have withered away and man will have moved from the realm of necessity to that of freedom. Once the triumph of socialism has inaugurated this happy time there will be a change, they recognize, in the character of literature. Georg Lukács, for example, writes: "The decisive distinction between socialism and all previous societies is that socialism aims to eliminate the antagonistic character of social contradictions. Literature has the immensely important task of describing this process, of exploring the problems thrown up by it. . . . If, however, the

2. *Utopian Fantasy* (London: Routledge & Paul, 1955), pp. 112–22.

elimination of this antagonistic character is seen as something immediately realizable, rather than as a process, both the antagonism and the contradiction, the motor of all development, will disappear from the reality to be depicted." Under socialism, says Lukács, "critical realism . . . will wither away."[3] Projections into this cloudless future sometimes have their comic side. A story is told that at a writers' conference in Moscow in the early 1930s André Malraux caused consternation by rising to ask, "What happens in a classless society when a streetcar runs over a beautiful girl?" Gorky was hauled out of a sick-bed to deliver the answer, arrived at after long debate: in a planned and classless society, a streetcar would not run over a beautiful girl.[4] Years before, Etienne Cabet's Icarians had come to similar conclusions; they had a law decreeing that there should be no accidents to pedestrians, whether caused by horses, vehicles, or anything whatever.

Under the new dispensation which eliminates conflict from society, the angularities of human character upon which the novel so much depends would inevitably be softened; diversity and eccentricity would tend to give way to homogeneity, humors to milder modulations on a temperate standard. This implies, of course, a very considerable melioration in the condition of men's lives;

3. Georg Lukács, *The Meaning of Contemporary Realism*, trans. John and Necke Mander (London: Merlin Press, 1963), pp. 120, 114–15. Cf. Herbert Marcuse, who suggests "the historical possibility of conditions in which the aesthetic could become a *gesellschaftliche Productivkraft* and as such could lead to the 'end' of art through its realization." *An Essay on Liberation* (Boston: Beacon Press, 1969), p. 45.

4. Michael Harrington tells the anecdote in *Cacotopias and Utopias*, the record of a conversation he had with W. H. Ferry and Frank L. Keegan (Center for the Study of Democratic Institutions, 1965), p. 21.

Brook Farm being what it was, Hawthorne had no such transformations to contend with in *The Blithedale Romance*. However, the narrator of Robert Graves's *Seven Days in New Crete* (1949) complains that the people of New Crete (a utopian community of the future), handsome and happy as they are, lack character. There are no congenital idiots or drunks among them, he admits, but the place and the people lack salt. In Hermann Hesse's *Magister Ludi*, the narrator asserts that for authors in the past "the important ingredients of a personality were deviation, abnormality and originality—often to the point of pathology—whereas we of today only speak of personalities when we meet with men who are beyond all originalities and peculiarities and who have succeeded in achieving the most perfect possible self-identification with the general." [5]

A society whose values are reflected in this kind of personality tends toward complete stasis. This has always been a problem for utopian writers, who have felt obliged to introduce conflict into their tales if they were to move at all. The usual device has been to import it from without: conflict, introspection, suffering, "character"—such as they are—usually arrive in Utopia with the visitor from outside. Lord Carisdale, in Etienne Cabet's *Voyage en Icarie* (1840), brings his sentimental entanglement with Miss Henrietta with him from England; Julian West's agonies in *Looking Backward* are his heritage from the nineteenth century; earthlings bring epidemics, both biological and moral, to Wells's utopia in *Men Like Gods*; B. F. Skinner's Frazier has personality problems because he was not born in Walden Two; Huxley's Pala is overcome by the barbaric world surrounding it. Utopia as such provides little opportunity for the progression

5. Originally published as *Das Glasperlenspiel* (1943); trans. Mervyn Savill (New York: F. Ungar, 1957), pp. 14–15.

by opposition we are accustomed to in literature and in life. When a killing occurs in Utopia—as in *News from Nowhere*—the violence is used, not as a structural element to provide necessary disequilibrium, but to demonstrate that even in arcadia men are still dashed about by their passions. Such events are very rare, though: utopia, in Claude Lévi-Strauss's terms, is, if not "cold," at least a "cool" society, almost unimaginable to us who live in societies superheated by progress.

Thus the more ideal the society depicted, the more unavailable will be the materials out of which novelists and writers of romance traditionally fashion their work. Insofar as the utopia is a fictional mode it obviously has many and interesting relations with the novel form, but it should not be thought of as somehow struggling to assimilate itself to that form. Ideally, at its loftiest and most pure, the utopia aspires to (if it has never reached) the condition of the idyll as Schiller describes it—that mode of poetry which would lead man, not back to Arcadia, but forward to Elysium, to a state of society in which man would be at peace with himself and the external world. The character of the idyll, says Schiller, is that it reconciles perfectly *"all opposition between actuality and the ideal,* which has supplied material for satirical or elegiac poetry." Its dominant tone would be calm, the calm that follows accomplishment and is accompanied by the feeling of an infinite power.[6]

Writers in the nineteenth century, particularly in France, attempted this assured and celebratory style with almost uniformly dreary results. A few, however— most notably William Morris—qualified the celebratory with infusions of the satiric. Their works (as suggested

6. "Naive and Sentimental Poetry," *Naïve and Sentimental Poetry and On the Sublime,* trans. and ed. Julius A. Elias (New York: F. Ungar, 1966), pp. 145–54.

in the first essay of this book) are structurally like the formal verse satire, with the proportions of positive and negative elements reversed; or they are like heroic poems of the seventeenth century which fitfully maintain a balance between panegyric and satire—between praise of virtue and the virtuous and sharp condemnation of virtue's enemies. In the twentieth century, however, the utopian balance—celebration of the achieved good place, on the one hand; exposure of the bad, on the other—has been disturbed, as it has proved nearly impossible to imagine the conditions which call for the celebratory style. Huxley attempts it—courageously, I think—in *Island*, with what success we shall consider in the next essay.

The fictional conventions of the utopia are far more stereotyped than are those of the novel. Consider *Gulliver's Travels*. In each of the four books the central character embarks on a voyage, lands alone in a strange country, makes contact with the inhabitants, learns about the customs and institutions of their land, makes certain comparisons with Europe, returns home. This is the prescriptive pattern of the genre. It admits, of course, of a good deal of variation, particularly in the journey (whether in space or time) into and out of utopia, and it may be dressed up with love stories, strange adventures, complications of various kinds; but the central element—the exposition of utopian life—is notoriously invariant. The archetypal gambit is More's at the end of book 1 of *Utopia*:

> Therefore, gentle Master Raphael, quoth I, I pray you describe unto us the island. And study not to be short, but declare largely in order their grounds, their rivers, their cities, their people, their manners, their ordinances, their laws, and, to be short, all things that you shall think us desirous to know. And you shall think us desirous to know whatsoever we know not yet.

Hythloday obliges at length, his discourse broken in only the most minimal way by queries or interjections from his auditors. Again, "Tell me how the magistrates are chosen," demands the Grand Master of the Knights Hospitalers of his guest, the Genoese sea captain, in Campanella's *City of the Sun*; and the captain responds appropriately. Almost two hundred and fifty years later: "Allons, Dinaros . . . expliquez à milord les merveilles qui sont une énigme pour lui; exposez-lui les principes de notre organisation *sociale* et *politique*; . . . milord ne sera pas le seul qui vous entendra avec plaisir."[7]

The pleasure palls, however, under this relentlessly mechanical approach to the necessary expository problem. Whereas Plato's dialogue in the *Republic* is a process of exploration and intellectual discovery, the creator of a fictional utopia presents us with a thing made—a new thing that must be explained. The technical problem has baffled even the best writers. William Morris, for example, clearly recognizes that old Hammond's long discourse in the middle of *News from Nowhere* is painfully wooden. It deals with the prescriptive materials: the customs, the mode of life, the politics ("we have none") of the new society and how these came about. The account of "How the Change Came" reflects Morris's own shattering experience of "Bloody Sunday" in Trafalgar Square (1887); but although his passion invigorates Hammond's discourse, the old man is allowed to go on far too long. In an attempt to break up this section, Morris shifts without warning from the normal question-and-answer expository mode—"I asked . . . He answered . . ."—to a dialogue form like that Diderot uses in the *Supplement to Bougainville's "Voyage"* (1796). The dialogue is static, however, and to alter the format of the

7. Etienne Cabet, *Voyage en Icarie*, 2d ed. (Paris: J. Mallet, 1842), p. 34.

page temporarily is not enough to lighten the heavy expository load. Splendid work that it is, *News from Nowhere* is irretrievably swaybacked, overborne by old Hammond's garrulity.

Still, the difficulty with this section of Morris's book is quantitative rather than substantive, for at the heart of any literary utopia there must be detailed, serious discussion of political and sociological matters. This seems to be inescapable and constitutes a major difference from the novel. F. R. Leavis is surely right to insist on the "elementary distinction to be made between the *discussion* of problems and ideas, and what we find in the great novelists." [8] The novelist's art is to metamorphose ideas into the idiosyncratic experience of complex human beings. For reasons advanced throughout this chapter, the utopian writer has rarely been able to accomplish this translation. Instead of incarnating the good life dramatically, novelistically, the characters of utopia discuss it. In part, this is a consequence of the fact that the fictional utopia is a bastard form, answering to the claims of a number of disciplines. It purports to present a more or less detailed picture of a society significantly better than that in which the writer lives. The nature of the enterprise inevitably elicits from the reader a series of questions: is the society depicted just? does it answer to legitimate human needs? would it work? would we like to live there? is the writer's criticism of his own society well taken? Because they are subject to the laws of politics, morality, sociology, economics, and various other fields, the issues to which these questions and dozens like them apply require discursive treatment. They belong to a reality foreign to that enacted in a novel. They are not literary issues, nor can the work which elicits and tries to

8. *The Great Tradition* (London: Chatto & Windus, 1948), p. 7.

answer questions about them be judged in terms applicable to the work of Henry James.

Most writers of fictional utopias have had far more interest in, and commitment to, the social-political aspects of their work than to the fiction, which they have considered largely instrumental—a means, not available to the philosopher, to "strike, pierce [and] possess the sight of the soul," as Sidney puts it in the *Apology for Poetry*. "But even in the most excellent determination of goodness," asks Sidney, "what philosopher's counsel can so readily direct . . . a whole commonwealth, as the way of Sir Thomas More's Utopia?" Still, if the poet has more force in teaching than the philosopher or historian, as Sidney maintains, utopian writers have in general lacked not only high poetic talent but even respect for the poet's art. Most have used the rather shoddy feigned images that came readily to them, content if the hackneyed presentation of a love affair would serve as bait while the social moral did its work. A world removed from Sidney's lofty vision, Edward Bellamy writes impatiently of his fable as sugar-coating designed to make his doctrine palatable. William Dean Howells wondered whether Bellamy's ethics would keep his aesthetics in remembrance.[9] It seems highly unlikely that they will; but there can be no doubt that Bellamy's aesthetics—that is, the elements of romance in his work—contributed heavily to the immense popular success of *Looking Backward*. This is a tribute to the raw power of fiction: the standards of the genre have not been high.

The relationship between the fictionality of utopias and the social ideas their authors want to express is likely to be fairly complex. Because the social dogmas and critiques are often radical and sometimes dangerous, the

9. Preface to Bellamy's *The Blindman's World* (Boston: Houghton, Mifflin, 1898), p. xiii.

unreality of the fiction may be insisted upon as protection to the author: the word *Utopia* means "no place"; *Hythloday* means "purveyor of nonsense"; and it is all only make-believe after all. More's position with respect to Utopian doctrines is, as a result of the cleverly manipulated fiction, highly ambiguous, which, given his political situation, was prudent. On the other hand, the fictionality of utopia is sometimes an embarrassment, particularly to nineteenth-century writers who are agonizingly convinced that the societies they have constructed in their heads are viable in the real world. They depict the imaginary society as graphically as possible, but then are afraid that the fictionality of the presentation may lead to dismissal of their ideas as unreal. The final section of *Voyage en Icarie* drops the fiction altogether; it is written in the first person by Cabet himself under the heading: "Explications de l'auteur.—Doctrine communitaire" and consists of a simple schematic resumé of the principles which have been enunciated at interminable length in Icaria. The book ends, not with the sentimental transports of Lord Carisdale, who has been forgotten, but with direct, urgent exhortation: reader, take these ideas seriously! Or again, Louis Sébastien Mercier in *L'An 2440* (1771) maintains, in his own person, a running footnote commentary on his text, pointing morals, lecturing his readers, making constant references to affairs of his own day—centuries removed, of course, from the time of his romance. Mercier attempts by his subtextual intrusion to anchor his fiction in reality. For these writers the fiction is a double-edged tool—a means to make the dream of utopia palpable, as Cabet says in his preface, but one which at the same time works against itself.

It has not always been clear exactly what the utopian writer's responsibility is to his fiction. Some sections of

Samuel Butler's *Erewhon*, for example, are straight essays critical of English customs and beliefs. They lie alongside the fiction, only the most minimal gesture having been made toward their incorporation; they are to be read in their own right as essays, not necessarily as integral parts of a fictional structure. Butler, of course, was perfectly aware of this and apologetic: "*Erewhon* was not an organized whole," he wrote in the preface to the revised edition; "there was hardly any story and little attempt to give life and individuality to the characters." Still, the fact remains, to which Butler points: *Erewhon Revisited* is structurally more of a piece than *Erewhon*, but *Erewhon* is the better reading of the two.

As these remarks indicate, Butler was concerned with problems of genre, although it cannot be said that he pushed hard at their solution. H. G. Wells was characteristically more energetic. His technical observations, and the experiments he undertakes, in *A Modern Utopia* (1905) are extremely interesting, even if, as he recognized, he did not make the aesthetic breakthrough he had hoped for. The formal premises of *A Modern Utopia* entail a distinction between Wells the author (who writes the first and last chapters of the work in italics) and an insistent Voice, issuing from a man looking remarkably like Wells, whom we are to imagine sitting at a table on stage, reading aloud from a manuscript about utopias. Behind the owner of the Voice (whom we might call "Wells") is a movie screen on which images intermittently appear. "Wells" we are to imagine as an actor in the film and a commentator on the action—in general, a philosophical guide. *A Modern Utopia* is an account of his adventures—alternately ratiocinative and physical—among utopian ideas and places. (The complexity of this situation—its use of film and commentator—may have suggested to Huxley the idea for the structure of *Ape and Essence*.)

The result is a hybrid form, part fiction—the adventures of "Wells" and his companion the botanist in Utopia—and part essay—the discursive explorations of "Wells" at his lecture table. "A Note to the Reader" (a preface to the prefatory chapter) explains how H. G. Wells, the author, arrived at this unusual form. In the course of presenting as lucid and entertaining a picture of Utopia as possible, he wanted to make a number of observations on economic and sociological matters. He rejected the form of the argumentative essay as too rigid. Similarly, he rejected straight narrative because it was inhospitable to the discussion of ideas. He considered making the work a "discussion novel" in the manner of Peacock's development of the philosophical dialogue; but that entailed unacceptable complications among the characters. He experimented with a form resembling that of Boswell's *Life of Johnson*, a play between monologue and commentator. Finally Wells settled on what he calls the "shot-silk texture" of his alternating fictional narrative and philosophical discussion—this last complete with footnote references to Hillquit's *History of Socialism in the United States* and an article in *Mind*. His technique is a sophisticated variant of the method Butler used in *Erewhon*.

Wells felt that the new form was the best he could find for the rather special purpose he had in mind. A bold, and in many ways an effective, conception, the boldness did not always carry over into execution. For example, Wells allowed the narrative sections of the work to be hampered by a clumsy entanglement with the subjunctive mood: all the adventures in Utopia are governed by the "Suppose that such-and-such were the case" of "Wells," the owner of the Voice. When in the first chapter "Wells" and the botanist (it is generically significant that he has no name) are translated in an instant from the Alps in Europe to the Alps in Utopia, the language fails to affirm the translation: "We should scarcely note the change. Not a cloud would have gone from the sky"—the subjunctive mood instead of "scarcely noted" and "had gone from the sky." Again, on the heels of one of the essay-sections, this: "After we have paid for our lunch in the little inn that corresponds to Wassen, the botanist and I would no doubt spend the rest of the forenoon in . . . discussion"—not, "we spent" the rest of the forenoon. . . . Shortly thereafter the indicative mood takes over as the action is dramatized; but then again, and throughout, the subjunctive reasserts itself. (The cinema, which we are to think of as depicting the narrative sections, has developed subtle techniques for projecting the subjunctive mood: did Wells have these in mind?)

It is as though Wells felt dependent on the subjunctive as mediator between the essayist Voice and the narrative adventure, as though he were not willing to commit himself completely to the fictional reality of Utopia—as though Utopia were a hypothesis rather than a place. This is surprising because in some sections of the book Wells is wonderfully assured in his use of fantasy. At one point the botanist delivers himself of his opinions on race: "'But you would not like,' he cried in horror, 'your daughter to marry a Chinaman or a negro!'" The response of "Wells" could not be more free: "It is my Utopia, and for a moment I could almost find it in my heart to spite the botanist by creating a modern Desdemona and her lover sooty black to the lips, there before our eyes." But this same assurance does not extend to the ontological status of Utopia; Wells holds back from giving it full imaginative reality.

For all his ingenuity Wells felt that the "conflicting form" he had devised could not finally dissolve the incompatibility of the materials he was working with: the large generalities of the ideas, the insistent specificity of the characters. When he focused on one element, the other grew vague and indistinct. This, he concluded, was a limiting condition of the genre:

> There must always be a certain effect of hardness and thinness about Utopian speculations. . . . That which is the blood and warmth and reality of life is largely absent; there are no individualities, but only generalized people. In almost every Utopia—except, perhaps, Morris's 'News from Nowhere'—one sees handsome but characterless buildings, symmetrical and perfect cultivations, and a multitude of people, healthy, happy, beautifully dressed, but without any personal distinction whatever. . . . This burthens us with an incurable effect of unreality.

"Wells," whose remarks these are, sees nothing to be done about it, nor, presumably, does his progenitor: "It is a disadvantage that has to be accepted."

If the writer of utopia could translate the ideas of his fiction into the experience of his characters, as the novelist does, then it would seem that he could escape from the thinness of which Wells complains. Clearly he can show human beings living in what he takes to be utopian conditions; but it appears to be almost impossible for him to create characters of any dimension who enact the constitutive ideas of utopia. He cannot make them *interesting*. Perhaps partly to avoid this dilemma Mary McCarthy, in *The Oasis* (1949), shifts her emphasis full on to character; that is, instead of showing in detail the problems of founding a utopian community and the principles by which it operates, she takes its establishment largely for granted (it is surprisingly successful, given the predilections of the author), then turns her cold eye on the New York intellectuals who make it up. The concentration on character and type makes for splendid satire—no question of dullness here—but thrusts the idea of utopia, whether positively or negatively conceived, well into the background.

Further difficulties, inherent in the form, prevent the utopia from achieving the kind of reality we know in the novel. Among them is the ancient and notorious problem of depicting the good. As a knowledgeable authority of our day, J. R. R. Tolkien, says in *The Hobbit*, "It is a strange thing, but things that are good to have and days that are good to spend are soon told about and not much to listen to." Untested goodness, unthreatened happiness are hard to make dramatic, and the *longueurs* of heaven have baffled the greatest writers. Thus utopias often seek to identify themselves negatively—"by contraries," as Gonzalo says in *The Tempest*—by dwelling on the vices and miseries they do not have, like angels contemplating the gridirons of hell. Swift's explanation, in the Preface to *A Tale of a Tub*, of the popularity of satire over panegyric is to the point: "For the materials of panegyric being very few in number, have been long since exhausted. For, as health is but one thing, and has been always the same, whereas diseases are by thousands, besides new and daily additions; so, all the virtues that have been ever in mankind, are to be counted upon a few fingers, but his follies and vices are innumerable, and time adds hourly to the heap." Utopia is a healthy society, its description soon exhausted; and happy families are all alike. In *News from Nowhere* old Hammond regrets that the youngsters of his day have little interest in the history of the past. "The last harvest, the last baby, the last knot of carving in the market place, is history enough for them." Splendid material for arcadian experience but quite intractable for the novel as we know it.

Some of the contradictions in Robert Graves's *Seven Days in New Crete* (1949; the American edition is called *Watch the North Wind Rise*) may well develop from Graves's restiveness under the formal and experiential limitations of utopia. New Crete has a good many straight utopian characteristics; that is, Graves presents in a favorable light most of the social, political, and religious arrangements of this society, visited in a dream of the future by Edward Venn-Thomas, a twentieth-century poet. Civilization has long before proved itself a catastrophe. New Cretans, in a planned regression to a pre-Trojan War state of culture, worship the White Goddess, practice magic, hold all necessities in common, and enjoy a notably undemocratic social system: they play their established roles in hierarchically ordered estates or classes modelled on (and containing some of the ambiguities of) Plato's Republic. Otherwise, however, they share with William Morris's Englishmen a contemptuous dislike for science and technology and a complementary passion for individually crafted objects: "nothing without the hand of love" is with them a religious principle.[10] New Cretans have been careful to preserve from the past no information on philosophy, advanced mathematics, physics, or chemistry; they retain no machinery more complicated than the pulley or lathe. Instead of industrialism, they have pageantry and ritual—in short, a society that in most respects Graves could be expected to approve. The narrator, however, finds life in New Crete "a little too good to be true." When Quant, a poet, admits that utopian existence is too easy to allow for the sterner satisfactions of more rugged eras, Venn-Thomas speaks favorably of Bernard Mandeville's principle that vice is necessary for the proper operation of a commonwealth. A bit of vice unquestionably makes Graves's narrative

10. What is utopian for writers like Morris, W. D. Howells (*A Traveller from Altruria* [1894]), W. H. Hudson, and Graves would be anathema to Cabet, Bellamy, Wells, and many others. Wells loathed the "toil may be made a joy" principle of Ruskin and Morris, the folly of rich men playing at life, he said. To him, bodily labor is a curse, as Hawthorne learned at Brook Farm; the machine can remove it. See *A Modern Utopia*, chap. 3, pt. 6.

task easier. He has the Goddess arbitrarily introduce evil into utopia in the form of sexual lust. The results are satisfactorily lurid: conflict, murder, even a couple fornicating on the victim's grave. Graves may have been led to these devices because he had trouble moving in the rarefied air of utopia; by injecting a more earthy atmosphere he kept the fiction going, but at the expense of the utopian premise.

Similarly, in *The Coming Race* (1871) Bulwer-Lytton found it difficult to make much of the lives of the Vril-ya, of whom all that could be said is, "they were born, they were happy, they died." Despite the superior felicity of their existence, the narrator concludes that any intelligent man from earth would die of ennui among them; and had it not been for the fantastic elements of his fiction, it is hard to see what would have spared Bulwer-Lytton's readers a similar fate. W. H. Hudson's protagonist Smith in *A Crystal Age* (1906) finds the happiness of the forest people a cruel trap when he learns that sexual love has been transcended into universal love; the prospect of a life of "chill moonlight felicity" appalls him as, with one part of his mind, it may have appalled his creator who believed in the creative function of passion and strife. In any event Smith longs for the power to shatter the idyllic world into which he has been introduced; he wants to repeople the land with the struggling, starving millions of the nineteenth century so that love, *real* love, may blossom once more.

Writers of the most diverse commitments have agreed on the dreary paradox that a life containing an overplus of good must be stupefyingly boring. It is pleasant to contemplate James Boswell, busy in Elysium, bringing Dr. Johnson and Bertolt Brecht together for discussion of this theme which is common to *Rasselas* and *The Rise and Fall of the City of Mahagonny*. Such unlikely agreements

may arise, however, less from the substantive merits of
the case than from the fact that except at the most primitive level we lack a language and conventions for depicting
man in a happy state. Schiller calls for an idyll in which
humanity is shown to be reconciled with itself, in the
individual as well as in the whole of society. Poets have
sometimes been able to express the first condition, but
not the second. "Who can describe . . . the happiness of
the Troglodytes?" asks Montesquieu's Usbek. A great
many have tried, but we still wait for an answer. Our
imagination of the good life is as barren as our imagination
of the bad is rich.

Negative utopias, which deal with a version of the bad
life, clearly offer the greater scope to fictional treatments
approaching the novelistic, although in fundamental ways
Zamyatin's *We* and Anthony Burgess's *A Clockwork
Orange* (1962) are as far removed from the novel proper
as are *News from Nowhere* and *Island*. The novel traditionally focuses on human character, in all its substantiality
and dimension, as it manifests itself in society. Negative
utopias depict a society in which human character can
hardly be said to exist at all. "Surely it is clear that
individual self-consciousness is only a disease," says
Zamyatin's D-503. The idea of the self as a unique and
inviolable entity is an anachronism in the worlds of *We*
and *1984*, a crime; to eradicate it is society's most compelling aim. I-330's claim that man is like a novel whose end
we do not know images perfectly her subversive function
in the United State. The characters of *We* are interesting,
as characters, precisely to the degree that they retain
certain atavistic qualities which throw them into conflict
with the orthodoxy of their world. It is a nice paradox
that D-503's hairy hands symbolize to him his connection
with the beast, but to us a quality that almost makes
him human. Thus negative utopias are best thought of,

not as novels, but as belonging to that tricky genre of which Wayne Booth speaks in his review of *Island*—the genre to which Northrop Frye has given the name Menippean satire or anatomy, after Robert Burton's exemplary work.[11] Frye's discrimination has been remarkably fruitful for criticism: the anatomy, he says, deals less with people as such than with characters acting as mouthpieces of ideas or mental attitudes. Writers in this genre make no attempt to create naturalistic human beings; their characters are stylized, mechanical, flat. The expectations we bring to the *Satyricon*, *Gargantua and Pantagruel*, *Candide*, Barth's *Giles Goat-Boy* are very different from those we bring to *Emma* or *Sons and Lovers*: it is pointless to require of *Brave New World* that it try to be what they are.

The normative utopia has a relationship to the novel precisely like that of the anatomy; that is, instead of the "pedants, bigots, cranks, parvenus, virtuosi, [and] enthusiasts" who people Menippean satire (a list to which we can add Zamyatin's Numbers and their progeny), utopia has its legislators, wise men, priests, workers, lovers, who exist as characters only to enact an allegory of the good life. We are as misguided to expect "roundness" and complexity in the characterization of Huxley's Dr. MacPhail in *Island* as in that of the numbers in *We*. But whereas Zamyatin has been able to create stylized characters—and a literary style—marvelously appropriate to the world he created, no model of comparable authority exists for depiction of the good life.

In addition to the generic difficulties discussed above, utopia suffers under another handicap: it is not a subject likely to attract gifted writers who feel passionately about literature, if for no other reason than that the status

11. *Anatomy of Criticism* (Princeton: Princeton University Press, 1957), pp. 308–12; see Irving Howe, "The Fiction of Anti-Utopia," *New Republic* (23 April 1962), pp. 15–16.

of literature in utopia is, at best, certain to be problematic.[12] Presumably the same substantive problems which
have plagued writers trying to imagine what utopia
would be like will face those who try, once utopian
conditions are established, to create their own literature.
Edward Bellamy, hearty in his confidence that literature
will flourish in utopia, faces the issue in *Looking Backward*:
the romancer, he says, will have to construct his tales
without benefit of the social texture given by "contrasts
of wealth and poverty, education and ignorance, coarse-
ness and refinement, high and low"; he will not be able
to draw on motives of "social pride and ambition, the
desire of being richer or the fear of being poorer";
there will be no "sordid anxieties of any sort for one's
self or others." Deprived of all this, the writer will, it is
true, have available to him "love galore," but love
unfretted by artificial social barriers. To create great
literature in these conditions, says Bellamy's spokesman,
Julian West, is like making bricks without straw, a reflection
with which writers of pre-utopian times would surely agree.
Bellamy's romancer Berrian somehow succeeded: Julian
West stayed up all night entranced, reading his *Penthesilia*;
but Berrian's achievement we must take on faith. In the same
way we must take on faith the prophecy of Charles
Fourier that by the time the earth has three billion inhabitants organized into phalansteries, there will normally be
thirty-seven million poets living who are the equal of
Homer and the same number of writers of comedy as
good as Molière. These are estimates, Fourier admits.[13]

12. On this theme, see Robert L. Stilwell, "Literature and Utopia:
B. F. Skinner's *Walden Two*," *Western Humanities Review* 18
(1964): 331–41.
13. Charles Fourier, *Théorie des quatres mouvements; Oeuvres
complètes*, 6 vols. (Paris: Librarie sociétaire, 1841–45), 1: 117;
quoted in Frank Manuel, *The Prophets of Paris* (Cambridge,
Mass.: Harvard University Press, 1962), p. 237.

B. F. Skinner, less manic, is still optimistic about the place of literature in utopia. Frazier, discussing the matter in *Walden Two*, admits that in a society imposing fewer frustrations than we now know, the character of literature may change: "I daresay a few first-rate sonnets would have remained unwritten had the lady yielded"; but when the necessities of life are easily obtained, he anticipates a great welling up of artistic interest. "We shall never produce so satisfying a world that there will be no place for art."

Although Frazier's prediction is not unreasonable, many writers are unable to share his cheer. Like heroism, great art may prove incompatible with the conditions of a stable and happy society. Eighteenth-century writers mourned the passing of the epic, but not the "barbaric" conditions which made the epic possible. Novelists— perhaps even painters—contemplating the putative state of their art under utopian conditions, face a similar dilemma. The narrator of Bulwer-Lytton's *The Coming Race* finds the portraits of the Vril-ya painted seven thousand years ago much superior to those of the last three thousand years; as features in the paintings appeared more serene, reflecting the increasing serenity of Vril-ya society, the art of the painter became tame and mono- tonous. As to literature, the Vril-ya have only an insipid poetry of description; because they no longer experience the passions which motivated the great poetry of the past, the Vril-ya have no subject.[14]

Not all writers, of course, find a prospective dilution of literature insupportable. The only character in *News from Nowhere* who bemoans the loss of vitality in the

14. The situation of the Vril-ya is like that of the writers in André Maurois's mock-utopia, *A Voyage to the Island of the Articoles* (1928), who are so pampered that they desert their wives in order to have something to write about.

novel under the new utopian conditions is Ellen's grandfather, the old grumbler who has a hearty dislike of
heaven. Ellen puts him straight. Perhaps books were
well enough in the past, she says, when they could palliate
the miseries of people's lives; but there is no place for
them today. "When will you understand that after all
it is the world we live in which interests us; the world of
which we are a part, and which we can never love too
much? Look!" she says, laying her hands on the shoulders
of the two lovers, "look! these are our books in these
days!"

Of the 274,000 books that Robert Graves's New
Cretans found had been written on Shakespeare, they
kept only 2, which they digested into three pages. In the
same spirit they tossed away all of Shakespeare's work
but what they considered the best: thirty pages in all.

> *Paper feeds on paper*
> *And on the blood of men.*
> *Engrave the durable*
> *On plates of gold and silver,*
> *Lest memory of it wavers. . . .*
> *Cretans, have done with paper*
> *And with parchment, its dour brother.*

Poetry, to be sure, is encouraged in New Crete, and
magical poetry, with power to blister a victim's cheek,
enthusiastically practiced; but almost nothing written is
kept, nor is it worth being kept. The ordered and serene
life of New Crete is incompatible with the thrilling
intensities of passion experienced by men in more turbu-
lent days and fixed in their poetry. Quant, a New Cretan
poet who knows about these matters, realizes, sadly,
that the time has passed when true poetry can be written
in his language. Graves's insistence on the theme shows
clearly that it is of genuine concern to him. It probably

accounts for some of his ambivalence toward the utopia he has created—an ambivalence reflected in the narrator's spasmodic attempts to assess the gains and losses associated with a life unmarked by poverty and crime.

For example, the worship of the goddess is the indispensable stabilizing force in New Crete. Venn-Thomas, the narrator, is horrified that the annual fertility rites include ritual murder and cannibalism; on the other hand, however, so awful is this sacrifice that New Cretans take no other human life whatever, even in war. Venn-Thomas makes the inevitable comparison: "I thought of the strewn corpses on Monte Cassino, where I had been almost the only unwounded survivor of my company; and of the flying-bomb raid on London, when I had held a sack open for an air-raid warden to shovel the bloody fragments of a child into it." A certain half-wittedness in respect to religion, Venn-Thomas decides, is indispensable to the good life, but he is perfectly willing to choose such half-wittedness over the whole-wittedness demanded by the American Century. ("Nor did Russia appeal to me in the least; the regime was anti-poetic.") Still, there *is* the decline of poetry in New Crete, and Venn-Thomas is as romantic a poet as is Graves, his creator. At the end, and with unmistakable relish, Venn-Thomas, swelled with a divine afflatus, prophesies the rising of the north wind in New Crete and a harvest of misery which will once more make possible the ecstasies of worship and of true poetry.

Brave New World, as might be expected, puts the issue of art and utopia with unpleasant clarity. Of course, says the Controller, *Othello* is better than the feelies; but social instability is a necessary condition of writing *Othello*, and the happiness of the new society cannot accommodate instability. "You've got to choose between happiness and . . . high art. We've sacrificed the high art."

Nobody would have suffered more acutely from the loss of high art than Aldous Huxley, yet when in *Island* he comes to describe happiness among the inhabitants of Utopia—a very different order of experience from happiness in the Brave New World—he presides over the demise of significant literature with savage zeal. Again the issue is starkly put: "Dualism. . . . Without it there can hardly be good literature. With it, there most certainly can be no good life." This is an aphorism from the notebook of the Old Raja containing the principles on which the Utopia of Pala is founded. Farnaby, the visiting journalist, pushes the implications to their limit: "if one's to believe your Old Raja literature is incompatible . . . with human integrity, incompatible with philosophical truth, incompatible with individual sanity and a decent social system, incompatible with everything except dualism, criminal lunacy, impossible aspiration, and unnecessary guilt." This formulation, more extravagant even than that in *Brave New World*, represents the thrust of Huxley's thinking shortly before his death. That he should have thought life more important than literature is surely not surprising. One thinks of Keats: poetry is "not so fine a thing as philosophy—For the same reason that an eagle is not so fine a thing as a truth." But that Huxley should allow literature to be rejected in such violent terms is a measure of his despair.[15] "Never mind," says Farnaby, grinning ferociously, "after Pala has been

15. Huxley's experiments with drugs contributed to his devaluation of the arts: "To a person [under the influence of mescalin] whose transfigured and transfiguring mind can see the All in every *this*, the first-rateness or tenth-rateness of even a religious painting will be a matter of the most sovereign indifference." Art, he says, is only for beginners, or for those resolute dead-enders who are content with the symbol rather than the thing symbolized, with the recipe rather than the actual dinner. *The Doors of Perception* (New York: Harper & Row, 1963), p. 29.

invaded and made safe for war and oil and heavy industry, you'll undoubtedly have a Golden Age of literature and theology." The conclusion is precisely that of Graves's book, the point of view reversed.

Pala's supreme art, Farnaby is told, one which can be practiced by anybody, is the art of adequately experiencing the world. It is a familiar theme: in Socrates' terms, the· superiority of experience over the representation of experience; in other terms, real gratification over the substitute gratification of which Freud spoke. "Nous ne voulons que du réel," say the utopians of Restif de la Bretonne's Mégapatagonia, as out of hand they condemn painting, drama, and poetry.[16] "These are our books," cries Ellen in *News from Nowhere*, embracing the lovers; she echoes the Mégapatagonians: "nos tableaux, ce sont nos beaux Hommes, nos belles Femmes que nous voyons tous les jours." Ever since Socrates, in the *Republic*, recommended crowning the mimetic artist with fillets of wool and escorting him to another city, the theme has echoed in utopian literature. Moreover, utopia's reality is not that with which our writers are engaged. If the triumph of the artist is, as Lionel Trilling has said, to shape the material of pain we all share, utopia tries to eradicate that pain. Its function is to lower the temperature of the culture, to reduce the amount of "history" in it; for history, we know, is equivalent to pain. Four hundred years ago Campanella's Captain, in *The City of the Sun*, could exult: "Oh if you only knew what they say from their astrology . . . concerning the coming age and the fact that our age has more history in it in a hundred years than the whole world in the preceding 4,000 years. . . ." But that was in another country, and today

16. *La Découverte australe par un homme-volant, ou Le Dédale français* (Leipsick [Paris], 1781), 3:503–4.

utopia (where it is still the subject of the literary imagination) desperately seeks less history out of fear of the age to come—and that means, necessarily, less literature. To the degree that a literary artist helps bring about the conditions of utopia, he contributes to the death—or at least to the severe debilitation—of his art. It is a genuine dilemma.[17]

Paul Valéry points out that H. G. Wells and Jules Verne, who brilliantly depict the technology of the future, make no attempt to imagine its art.[18] As the *Nautilus* cruises at the bottom of the sea, Captain Nemo plays Bach, not the work of electronic composers. Certain writers attracted to utopia, however, have tried to visualize Valéry's "yet unknown kind of aesthetics"—in effect, like Julian West but with utterly different results, they have read *Penthesilia* by Berrian, Edward Bellamy's novelist of the future. Their rejection of the utopian enterprise is a critique of utopian art.

17. Dennis Gabor thinks the dilemma largely responsible for what he rashly speaks of as a new *trahison des clercs*—"the hostility of many artists to the future." *Inventing the Future* (London: Secker & Warburg, 1963), pp. 16, 168–69.

18. "Our Destiny and Literature," in *History and Politics*, trans. Denise Folliot and Jackson Mathews: vol. 10 of *Collected Works*, ed. Jackson Mathews (New York: Random House, 1962), pp. 181–82.

❧ 7 ❧

Anti-Anti-Utopia

Walden Two *and* Island

Against the optimistic utopias of the nineteenth century, *Erewhon* stands eccentric and interesting, modern in its alienation, its rejection of the dominant mystique of the age. "Do not machines eat as it were by mannery?" Today, almost overwhelmed in the flood of black visions of the future, two positive utopias, alienated from alienation, ask questions of our time as urgent as those of Butler. B. F. Skinner's *Walden Two* (1948) and Aldous Huxley's *Island* (1962) are daring ventures, full against the dominant imagination of the twentieth century. Perhaps only one as contemptuous of history as Skinner or one as desperately conscious of history as Huxley could have made the plunge. In any event, *Walden Two* and *Island* are our utopias, the two post-modern visions of the good place that speak most cogently against despair. Inevitably, Dostoevski's Grand Inquisitor hovers over both.

Skinner, an eminent behavioral psychologist turned writer of fiction, deliberately evokes the Grand Inquisitor *topos* by his delineation of T. E. Frazier, also a behavioral psychologist, the guiding genius of the fictional community called Walden Two. The community has the traditional utopian aim: the happiness of its members, the achievement of the Good Life. Unembarrassed by philosophical complexities, Frazier has no doubts about what the good life consists of: health, a minimum of unpleasant labor, the chance to exercise talents and abilities, full opportunity to develop intimate and satisfying personal relationships, plenty of relaxation and rest. To this unquestionably attractive goal Frazier adds another constituent: freedom from the responsibility of planning and making choices. Most people, he says, are content with day-to-day happiness as long as they are assured that they will be decently provided for. The theme is familiar; Frazier's "most people" are the millions of Dostoevski's legend. Walden Two has also its complementary elite, the highly intelligent few attracted by power, challenged by complex problems and distant goals—those who guard the mystery:

> "What remains to be done?" [Frazier] said, his eyes flashing. "Well, what do you say to the design of personalities? Would that interest you? The control of temperament? Give me the specifications, and I'll give you the man! What do you say to the control of motivation, building the interests which will make man most productive and most successful? Does that seem to you fantastic? Yet some of the techniques are available, and more can be worked out experimentally. Think of the possibilities! A society in which there is no failure, no boredom, no duplication of effort! . . . Let us control the lives of our children and see what we can make of them."

The priesthood of Walden Two will be as powerful as that of the legend.

Frazier is no more in doubt about the means of achieving the good life than about its ends. All that is required is intelligence together with what he loosely calls the experimental method, and the systematic application of well-known principles of behavioral engineering. If one wants a good society, he argues, one must answer two questions. One must discover what constitutes the best behavior of the individual from the point of view of the group concerned. Then one must determine how to induce the individual to behave in the desired way. These are experimental questions in process of being answered at Walden Two. Human engineering in this utopia starts with babies, all of whom are brought up communally under controlled conditions which preclude frustration, anxiety, fear. Gradually obstacles and annoyances are introduced into the babies' experience; they learn progressively how to cope with these unpleasant experiences so that what appears to be a slightly fiendish torture of children is in fact a method insuring that they will develop extraordinary tolerance for the frustrations they are bound to encounter in later life. Possibilities, the Planners claim, are boundless: destructive and wasteful emotions can be trained out of children, their self-control enhanced, the chances that they will be unhappy immeasurably lessened. All this—Walden Two's ethical training—is accomplished by the age of six.

Adults too can be conditioned to socially desirable behavior. Frazier explains: "if it's in our power to create any of the situations which a person likes or to remove any situation he doesn't like, we can control his behavior. When he behaves as we want him to behave, we simply create a situation he likes, or remove one he doesn't like. As a result, the probability that he will behave that way again goes up, which is what we want. Technically it's called 'positive reinforcement.'" The great power of the method lies in the fact that there is no restraint and no reason for revolt. "By a careful cultural design, we control not the final behavior, but the *inclination* to behave —the motives, the desires, the wishes." In short, the aim of Walden Two is to bring about the state of affairs H. G. Wells dreamed of: "every man doing as it pleases him, and none pleased to do evil." Does the system work? Look, says Frazier expansively, with all the self-confidence of a man who fears no contradiction, look how happy they are.[1]

Systematic conditioning of human beings is of course incompatible with the doctrine of human freedom, as Frazier's interlocutors observe. On this issue Frazier is as forthright as the Grand Inquisitor or Mustapha Mond. He denies that freedom exists at all. He has to deny it, for if man is free, then a technology of human behavior is impossible. As Dr. Johnson says, "The caprices of voluntary agents laugh at calculation." Frazier admits (as does Skinner elsewhere) that he cannot prove the nonexistence of freedom, but his science demands the assumption: "You can't have a science about a subject matter which hops capriciously about."[2] The justification for the

1. Donald C. Williams is outraged at Skinner's use of this bit of behavioral engineering ("The Social Scientist as Philosopher and King," *Philosophical Review* 58 [1949]; 348); but it is a device, perfectly appropriate to the genre, that has been exploited since Raphael Hythloday proved his case by pointing to the happiness of the Utopians. Skinner tries to use the same device, however, in a debate. He quotes a number of hostile reviews of *Walden Two*, then says: "One would scarcely guess that the authors are talking about a world . . . where . . . people are truly happy, secure, productive, creative, and forward-looking." This kind of reification outside the fictional frame is comically illegitimate as a way of arguing. For Skinner's remarks, see Carl R. Rogers and B. F. Skinner, "Some Issues Concerning the Control of Human Behavior," *Science* 124 (1956): 1059.

2. In *Science and Human Behavior* (New York: Macmillan, 1953), Skinner says that order is a working assumption of his scientific

controls of Walden Two is that *all* men are conditioned by their environment, normally in a random, haphazard, wasteful way. As Frazier says repeatedly, there is no virtue in accident. If personal freedom is an illusion and the control of behavior inevitable, it is far better that control be exercised rationally in the interests of social well-being, than that it fall into the hands of charlatans and demagogues. Furthermore Walden Two eschews the use of force and punishment; it is "free," that is, of those restraints, and in that sense is "the freest place in the world." The members of Walden Two *feel* free—a result of their conditioning—no matter how rigidly controlled they are. They do what they want to do, but, says Frazier, "we see to it that they will want to do precisely the things which are best for themselves and the community." Like Christians who act in accordance with God's plan, "their behavior is determined, yet they're free." All this is so close to Ivan Karamazov's legend that it can hardly be accidental. "Today," says the Grand Inquisitor to Christ in the long monologue, "people are more persuaded than ever that they have perfect freedom, yet they have brought their freedom to us and laid it humbly at our feet. But that has been our doing."

In other ways too Skinner brings Frazier and Walden Two within the orbit of Dostoevski's theme. One of man's greatest longings, says the old Inquisitor, is to be united in the universal harmony of an anthill. Skinner accepts the challenge of the image and allows Professor Augustine Castle, Frazier's antagonist in the fiction, to use it ("Walden Two is a marvel of efficient coordination—as efficient as an anthill") in his contemptuous characterization

---

enterprise "which must be adopted at the very start. We cannot apply the methods of science to a subject matter which is assumed to move about capriciously. . . . we must assume that behavior is lawful and determined" (p. 6).

of the community. And like the Grand Inquisitor, Frazier has no compunction about being the God of God: "I like to play God," he says; and he judges his own creation of Walden Two an improvement in some respects over the work of Genesis. As for his motivation, it is that of the Inquisitor: "These are my children, Burris. . . . I *love* them."

Still, these are not, one must recognize, the same children that the Grand Inquisitor loves: Skinner has carefully rejected certain elements of the legend. Part of the behavioral design at Walden Two insures that the Planners receive no adulation, no marks of honor or gratitude or special esteem, quite in contrast to the reverential awe accorded the Guardians of Ivan Karamazov's tale. And while Frazier may be identified with the unhappy elite of the legend, his unhappiness comes not from taking on the curse of the knowledge of good and evil, but because he is a product of twentieth-century society at large; Frazier was not born in Walden Two. His successors, the Planners of the future, not being so handicapped, will presumably not suffer his disability. All will be happy, even those who rule, in that blessed day.

Skinner handles these thematic intricacies with considerable skill, inviting the identification with the Grand Inquisitor, accepting some of the consequences of the identification, rejecting others, and positively revelling in the bathos involved. It is unnerving to recognize that "mystery," one of the three great powers with which Satan tempted Christ in the wilderness, is reduced by Skinner to a lollipop hung around the neck of a child. But then Frazier speaks of Jesus as a behavioral engineer and says of love, in a moment of high seriousness, that it is another name for positive reinforcement. Presumably Skinner thinks the shock value of such identifications compensates for their vulgarity.

Humanist critics of *Walden Two* have been so dismayed by Skinner's vision of the good life and so enraged by his evident contempt for their values and their disciplines that they have belabored him with every handle in the book, whatever its legitimacy as a weapon. Frazier says many outrageous things and so from another point of view does his antagonist, Professor Castle; but no matter who the speaker and what the circumstance, any opinion uttered is likely to be charged against Skinner himself. The temptation is admittedly strong in Frazier's case; most of the time he unquestionably expresses Skinner's own views, sometimes in language straight out of Skinner's textbooks. And Skinner's attempt to identify himself (Burrhus Frederick Skinner) with Professor Burris, the pallid narrator of the tale for whose soul Frazier struggles, is an engagingly ineffectual bit of behavioral engineering. But critics are irresponsible not to recognize that Skinner is aware of Frazier's messianic ambitions and that formally, at least, he puts ironic distance between himself and some of Frazier's most egregious pronouncements. This is a mild matter at times, as when Frazier, in a fit of enthusiasm, declaims: "The one thing that I would cry from every housetop is this: the good life is waiting for us—here and now!" Burris comments dryly: "I almost fancied I heard a Salvation Army drum throbbing in the distance." It is of considerable consequence, however, that Skinner portrays Frazier as a man driven by a desire to play God. Twice Skinner associates Frazier with the devil; and the scene in which Frazier takes Burris high on a hill to a rock formation called the Throne, where Frazier can overlook what he has created, sets unmistakable countercurrents to work:

"It must be a great satisfaction," I said finally. "A world of your own making."

"Yes," he said. "I look upon my work and, behold, it is good. . . ."

I reflected that his beard made him look a little like Christ. Then, with a shock, I saw that he had assumed the position of crucifixion.

I was extraordinarily ill at ease. . . . for all I knew, the man beside me might be going mad.

"Just so you don't think you're God," I said hesitantly. . . .

"There's a curious similarity," he said.

Without making excessive claims for the passage, one recognizes a genuine attempt to convey complexity; in ideological analyses of the book it should be respected.[3]

Skinner is perfectly aware of the equivocal nature of these matters. In the following passage he allows Frazier to utter sentiments revealing his arrogant ignorance of major political and philosophical issues, his tyrannical ambitions, his grotesque pride:

"Dictatorship and freedom—predestination and free will," Frazier continued. "What are these but pseudo-questions of linguistic origin? When we ask what Man can make of Man, we don't mean the same thing by 'Man' in both instances. We mean to ask what a few men can make of mankind. And that's the all-absorbing question of the twentieth century. What kind of world can we build —those of us who understand the science of behavior?"

"Then Castle was right. You're a dictator, after all."

"No more than God. Or rather less so."

Burris's response—"You're a dictator, after all"— sets distance between author and character. It is designed to reassure us: Skinner could not approve Frazier's

3. Even writers as sophisticated as Joseph Wood Krutch lose perspective in discussing *Walden Two*. Krutch writes of Frazier as though he were a self-actuating person who finds himself compelled to make a significant confession, i.e., that he likes power. The only one who can compel Frazier to do anything is Skinner, the author; and the confession is there for a purpose. See Krutch, *The Measure of Man* (Indianapolis, Ind.: Bobbs-Merrill, 1954), p. 60.

sentiments. And possibly he does not. But at the end of the book any distance between him and Frazier is effectively dissolved by Burris's conversion. Burris leaves Walden Two headed back for his job at the university; but only a few hours' exposure to life outside Utopia is enough to nauseate him. He returns to Walden Two on foot, a pilgrim. Not without apprehensions, however: "I glanced fearfully upward toward the Throne. There was no one there. . . . Frazier was not in his heaven. All was right with the world."

These are the last lines in the book. We are to share Burris's relief: Frazier is not really a dictator, which means somehow, that all is well. How risky it is! Whether Frazier is on the Throne or not, his ideas will continue to reign at Walden Two. Human beings will be treated according to the assumption (an assumption not capable of proof) that individual freedom does not exist, and they will be conditioned in such a way as to insure the accuracy of the assumption. Clearly, however, even if man is not free, there are degrees of nonfreedom; Frazier proposes to foster the illusion of freedom while actually increasing nonfreedom. Given his system, everything will depend upon the character of the conditioners (and those who condition them): if they are decent, humane men, possibly the good life will burgeon at Walden Two; if they are demagogues and tyrants, against whom Frazier warns, the potentialities of development have been fully mapped in the life as well as the literature of the twentieth century. The implication to be drawn from the last paragraph of *Walden Two* is that, had Frazier been on the Throne, Walden Two would have developed into a tyranny. Skinner seems not to recognize what a near thing it was.

In Aldous Huxley's *Island*, Will Farnaby, cynical journalist shipwrecked on the shores of Utopia, visits a Palanese couple for lunch. Shanta is breast-feeding her baby. Vijaya, the father, caresses the baby's back, then brings a large parrot into contact with the infant's body, moving the feathers gently back and forth on the brown skin. "Polly's a good bird," he chanted. "Polly's a very good bird."

"Such a good bird," Shanta whispered, taking up the refrain. "Such a *good* bird."

Vijaya explains to Farnaby that as a result of this training the Palanese get on beautifully with the local fauna—and, since appropriate modifications are made in the formula—with each other. The technique was picked up, Vijaya explains, over a hundred years ago from a tribe in New Guinea that believed in love and, unlike Christians and Buddhists, had invented a practical way of assuring that its people did, in fact, love one another:

> "Stroke the baby while you're feeding him; it doubles his pleasure. Then, while he's sucking and being caressed, introduce him to the animal or person you want him to love. Rub his body against theirs; let there be a warm physical contact between child and love object. At the same time repeat some word like 'good.' At first he'll understand only your tone of voice. Later on, when he learns to speak, he'll get the full meaning. Food plus caress plus contact plus 'good' equals love. And love equals pleasure, love equals satisfaction."
> "Pure Pavlov" [, said Farnaby].
> "But Pavlov purely for a good purpose. Pavlov for friendliness and trust and compassion. Whereas you prefer to use Pavlov for brainwashing, Pavlov for selling cigarettes and vodka and patriotism. Pavlov for the benefit of dictators, generals, and tycoons."

Vijaya's argument is precisely that of Frazier in *Walden Two*: the techniques of behavioral engineering are known and used constantly, most of the time by unscrupulous persons for evil ends. In a rational society they would be used systematically for good ends: as they are in Walden Two, as they are on Pala—as they were in the original *Utopia* itself: "for they use with very great endeavour and diligence to put into the heads of their children, whiles they be yet tender and pliant, good opinions and profitable for the conservation of their weal-public. Which, when they be once rooted in children, do remain with them all their life after and be wondrous profitable for the defence and maintenance of the state of the commonwealth. . . ."

Still, it is impossible to read of conditioned love in Pala without being aware of the ghastly possibilities; one remembers the Deltas being conditioned to hate flowers in the Neo-Pavlovian Conditioning Rooms of the Brave New World, and one remembers the hypnopaedic techniques ("I'm really awfully glad that I'm a Beta") which guarantee that the mind *is* precisely what has been implanted by the State. Other writers may have plunged more deeply into these grotesqueries than Huxley; they may have been more apocalyptic, more "novelistic" than he; but Huxley's is unquestionably the authoritative literary image of conditioned happiness and its horrors. How disconcerting then—but how logical, after all— to find in *Island*, Huxley's last despairing stab at showing what a good life might be in our time, some of the same conditioning methods (much less systematically applied, of course) that he had made notorious in *Brave New World*.

The issue comes up repeatedly in *Island*. Twenty percent of the population anywhere, Huxley claims, is highly suggestible, to the point where they are easy prey of propagandists. On Pala these potential somnambulists are identified as children; they are hypnotized and given special training so that they will not be hypnotizable later by enemies of liberty—the tyrant's technique used for socially benign ends. Again, a major characteristic of the religious and sensual life of Pala is the use of a psychedelic drug whose effect is to induce an experience of self-transcendence akin to that of the mystics. This is a far cry from the *soma* of *Brave New World* or the drugs often encountered in early utopias;[4] Huxley's tone is reverential as he describes the *moksha*-medicine and its uses. Doctor MacPhail in *Island* expresses Huxley's sentiments when he argues that the medicine connects the individual mind with Mind. The experience of the drug, he says, is like that of music, but incomparably more important: "the experience can open one's eyes and make one blessed." Psychedelic drugs are an essential element in Huxley's imagination of the good life; he seeks to accommodate this mechanical operation of the spirit into his search for the modalities of a free society. That he is groping for incompatibles, that he commends social practices that violate his earnest and repeatedly-expressed commitment to individual freedom, need not surprise us.

Huxley was caught up in what Whitehead forty years ago, in *Science and the Modern World*, identified as a radical inconsistency at the basis of modern thought. With one part of our minds we embrace a "scientific" view of man according to which man's total behavior is determined by prior causation. With another part of our minds—in our practical, everyday political lives—we insist that man is self-determined, autonomous, that he is free. The success of the behaviorists in treating man as a machine makes increasingly credible the postulate that man's freedom is a fiction. On the other hand, we know by our own most authentic experience the reality of existential choice. Put in these terms, the two positions

4. For example, in *La Terre australe connue* (1676) by Gabriel de Foigny the hermaphroditic inhabitants of Australia eat a "fruit of repose" which banishes melancholy and makes the blood dance in the veins.

are incompatible and, as Whitehead and many others have noted, modern thought is enfeebled thereby.

Thomas Henry Huxley, Aldous Huxley's grandfather, once claimed that he would be willing to be turned into a kind of clock, and wound up every morning, on condition that some great power would always make him think what is true and do what is right. He was not at all interested in the freedom to be wrong. Aldous Huxley sometimes writes in similar terms: "If only all of us . . . could be effectively filled, during our sleep, with love and compassion for all!" A man willing to be filled in this way is likely to entertain ideas about filling others. That men can be so filled—so conditioned—Huxley, of course, had not the slightest doubt. He criticized B. F. Skinner's technical work, not because in denying man's freedom Skinner proceeded from a false assumption, but because the work centered too narrowly on behavior and ignored biological differences in human beings. Huxley makes this point in several essays and again (without mentioning Skinner) in *Island*, where Doctor MacPhail is contemptuous of both the Freudian and the behaviorist schools of psychology. An inference to be drawn is that if the Pavlovians would incorporate biochemical sophistication into their discipline, their ability to control behavior would be unlimited.

Huxley's experiments with drugs toward the end of his life convinced him that, as he said, the pill is mightier than sword or pen; the dictatorships of the future, he predicted, will use the pill to bring men happiness—no less real experientially for being chemically induced—and to deprive them of their freedom. On the other hand, if pharmacology is a threat to freedom, it can also be used to heighten vigor and increase intelligence, man's greatest bulwarks against tyranny. By appropriate biochemical methods, says Huxley, "we can transform [adults and children] into superior individuals."[5] In this mood Huxley plays God in a way he normally deplores, "filling" others for their own good—his tone indistinguishable from that of Skinner at his most manic, the problem of freedom forgotten.

The opposing position in Huxley's dialogue with himself is put most forcibly by the Savage of *Brave New World*, who, like Dostoevski's Underground Man, opts for misery, pain, suffering in order to prove that he is not the keys of a piano—not the slave of a meretricious happiness. The Savage does not, however, speak for Aldous Huxley who, while ordinarily holding freedom to be a supreme value, rejects the exaggerated terms in which the dilemma is put in *Brave New World*. In most of his writing Huxley makes the elementary distinction between a systematic conditioning imposed scientifically on the individual citizen in a closed society (as in *Brave New World*) and the kind of conditioning to which every man is subject by virtue of having been born into a particular society at a particular time. The difference is that, although every man is a prisoner of his culture, he can, by an extraordinary act of will, escape from that prison into freedom of a kind—a manifest impossibility in the closed society. Huxley speaks of the great paradox of human life: "It is our conditioning which develops our consciousness; but in order to make full use of this developed consciousness, we must start by getting rid of the conditioning which developed it."

When he writes specifically of the ancient metaphysical problem of freedom of the will, Huxley equivocates. One can see this most clearly in the essay on Pascal.

5. "Drugs That Shape Men's Minds," *Collected Essays* (New York: Harper, 1959), pp. 336 ff. I want to thank Dr. Robert Lynch of La Jolla for enlightening discussion of the ideas of his close friend Aldous Huxley.

Huxley argues that most philosophical positions are no more than rationalizations of prevailing psychological moods. "Even the doctrines of 'fixed fate, free will, foreknowledge absolute,' for all the elaborateness of their form, are in substance only expression of emotional and physiological states. One feels free or one feels conditioned. Both feelings are equally facts of experience. . . ." The question of truth or falsity simply does not arise. Our grandparents, says Huxley, had to have things one way or the other—the world according to science or the world according to art—and they suffered excruciatingly thereby. We need not take so tragic a view of things. Given the state of our knowledge, one world view (the scientific as opposed to the mystical, for example) cannot be truer than another; philosophical consistency therefore (except in logic and epistemology) no longer has merit.

In this way Huxley comes to terms with the radical inconsistency in modern thought that exercised Whitehead. As with the contradictory theories of light with which physicists have had to come to terms, this solution, at the level of abstract thought, does not solve; but as an exercise of negative capability the equivocation allowed Huxley to live with a contradiction that cut at the heart of his engagement with man and society.

Island reflects his equivocation. Pala will be destroyed, predicts the Savonarolan Mr. Bahu, because it is too perfect—because it is successfully designed "to make every man, woman, and child on this enchanting island as perfectly free and happy as it's possible to be." Of course, not even on Pala are perfect happiness and perfect freedom possible. Mortality inevitably shadows happiness: people die on Pala, not of poverty or war or preventible disease—they die, in Michael Harrington's phrase, of death, which gives mortality a peculiar poignancy. Similarly, one cannot speak of a society as perfectly free which systematically uses hypnotism on children to alter character structure. It is possible to debate endlessly the degree of deprivation of individual freedom involved in Pavlovian methods of child raising and the dangers of tyrannical control entailed by the socially sanctioned use of psychedelic drugs. Still, Mr. Bahu's praise of Pala, like Huxley's intent in depicting Palanese society, was confined to the realm of the possible. That a society devoted to freedom of the individual should use in the service of its ends some of the techniques of unfreedom involves a contradiction obvious to the point of banality. The contradiction may, however, be necessary.

Walden Two and *Island* take the precarious state of twentieth-century Western society largely for granted; they were constructed, that is, with no sense that they had to be justified, like so many utopias, by spelling out in detail the wickedness and folly of our age. Both authors recognize that the time is late for such specification and that the telling might prove tedious as well as redundant. An ancient Irish apocalyptic tale foretells an age of doom characterized, in part, by the fact that every man shall have his own satirist. That time has surely come upon us; every man—and every child—is engaged in satire today. *Walden Two* and *Island* are fresh and interesting in that, although casting a negative light on our society, they are not *Brave New World* and *1984* writ again. When they portray utopia—battered word!—they mean it.

Walden Two makes some point of not being satirical at all. According to Frazier the Planners deliberately refrain from ridiculing the stupidities of the world outside, almost as though the target were too easy. Still, the traditional motivation for utopia is present: "Our civilization is running away like a frightened horse," says Frazier, recommending that we abandon it. At every point thoughout the development of our knowledge of Walden Two a contrast with the inferior world we know is either stated or implied, as when Steve Jamnik and Mary Grove, working-class visitors to Utopia, compare the richly satisfying married life they could have there with the dreary prospect awaiting them outside: a couple of rooms somewhere across the tracks, where the Irish kids clobber the Jews.

The most effective episode of this kind is at the end. Burris and Professor Castle are at the railroad station awaiting transportation home. Castle's imperceptive criticisms of Walden Two bring Burris's musings about the place into focus. Suddenly Burris finds himself ducking out on his tiresome colleague for a walk in the neighborhood of the station:

> I emerged into a blighted area in which rows of decaying stores had been converted into squalid living quarters. Dirty children played in dirty streets, tired and unkempt women leaned on window sills, hopeless men stood about in sullen groups. But I drew no comparison with Walden Two. The contrast was too massive to fit into the delicate play of forces in my mind. Walden Two had nothing in common with the human devastation about me now. It was absurd to ask which life one would choose, if these were the alternatives.

A headline in a newspaper catches his attention:

DIGNITY OF MAN
BACCALAUREATE
ADDRESS THEME

The president of Burris's university has been delivering a recent version of his standard speech, replete with every cliché in the repertoire of bankrupt humanism. The empty phrases represent to Burris the fecklessness, the futility, of education in a society lost beyond redemption. They trigger his decision to return to the hope of Walden Two.

The scene is modeled after *Looking Backward*, after the nightmare return of Julian West to the Boston of his birth. West finds the degradation and misery of the 1880s an absolute inferno after the antiseptic affluence of the year 2000. In what has become a standard gambit of utopian fiction, he reads a newspaper crawling with stories of war, strikes, unemployment, robbery, murder, and he sees with fresh eyes how industrialism has brutalized the urban poor. Bellamy pushes his rhetoric hard in this climactic episode, the most powerful scene in the book. Skinner's handling of the return of Burris is more restrained, but has something of the same effect. Given the context, Skinner has only (while disavowing any intent of comparison) to provide a brief glimpse of a major failure of our society, to print a couple of phrases from the baccalaureate address—"restoring the dignity of the human soul"—for the satirical point to be made.

Still, *Walden Two* contains very little overt satire. Professor Augustine Castle is a butt, his pomposities designed to discredit academic philosophy in general; and Frazier himself is caught out in his own arrogance once or twice. But this is minor. The ugly truths about society that, in fiction of this kind, satire would normally expose are simply taken for granted in *Walden Two*. On the third page, Steve Rogers, just back from the war, says almost casually to Professor Burris: "there are a lot of things about the way we are living now that are completely insane. . . ." That is what lies behind the book.

Aldous Huxley tested the idea of utopia more thoroughly than any other literary man of our day. *Brave New World* is utopia in caricature, a satire on the idea of utopia and our distortions of it. It is the classic warning of the abyss that lies at the end of our simplistic search for happiness. *Ape and Essence* (1948) is Huxley's dystopia, his *1984*, a hideous picture of the United States after the next nuclear war. The book is an unrecognized parent of currently popular black humor, its ferocious satire relieved occasionally by grotesque flashes of comedy. *Island*, Huxley's last book, reverses the negative progress, presenting itself as an image of sanity and health, the island of Pala as an oasis of humanity in a wilderness of monkeys. The three works, poignant reflections of Huxley's deepest concerns, form a unit.

In *Ape and Essence* a conversation between Dr. Poole and Belial's Arch-Vicar identifies the sources of Belial's triumph in the twentieth century:

"And then," says Dr. Poole. . . . "He [Belial] persuaded each side to take only the worst the other had to offer. So the East takes Western nationalism, Western armaments, Western movies and Western Marxism; the West takes Eastern despotism, Eastern superstitions and Eastern indifference to individual life. In a word, He saw to it that mankind should make the worst of both worlds."

"Just think if they'd made the best!" squeaks the Arch-Vicar. "Eastern mysticism making sure that Western science should be properly used; the Eastern art of living refining Western energy; Western individualism tempering Eastern totalitarianism." He shakes his head in pious horror. "Why, it would have been the kingdom of heaven."[6]

As so often in Huxley, the positive is defined in words uttered by the devil. Here the Arch-Vicar provides the ideological outline of *Island*, which is Huxley's major effort to work out in detail the normative element, the standard, of his satire—in some sense (although his

6. *Ape and Essence* (New York: Harper, 1948), p. 184.

standards changed), all his satire, from the beginning. Among other things, *Island* is the "third alternative" that Huxley once contemplated if he should ever rewrite *Brave New World*: the society of "freely co-operating individuals devoted to the pursuit of sanity" that he considered allowing the Savage to experience before ·being transported to "Utopia." In 1946, when Huxley broached the possibility of the third alternative, the word "utopia" was still equivalent in his mind to hell, although he was obviously thinking of the terms in which an imaginary good place might be described. Pala is that place, just as it is the secular kingdom of heaven of which Belial speaks with horror.

Although the emphasis is strongly on the normative in *Island*—on the institutions and beliefs and relationships that constitute Good Being on the island of Pala—the book inevitably contains some of Huxley's characteristic negative orientation. He sets up familiar targets for satiric treatment once more: Calvinism, for example, or styles in American consumer taste as exemplified in a Sears Roebuck catalog: "Soft Platform Wedgies in Wide Widths." The most interesting use of satire in *Island*, however, is as a test of Palanese values. Positive utopias have in their purity often been highly vulnerable to satire and irony. Huxley deliberately makes Farnaby, his central character, a satirist of sorts. Farnaby is a disillusioned journalist with a "flayed smile," a true Huxley—Graham Greene type, forever on the verge of nausea. Confronted by Pala's extraordinary combination of Western science and Eastern concern for human and spiritual values, Farnaby reacts true to his kind: he is the man who won't take yes for an answer. In the scene referred to earlier where Shanta is suckling her baby, Farnaby sits down beside the pair and begins stroking the child's body.

"This is another man," Shanta whispered. "A good man, baby. A *good* man."

"How I wish it were true!" he said with a rueful little laugh.

"Here and now it *is* true." And bending down again over the child, "He's a good man," she repeated. "A good good man."

He looked at her blissful, secretly smiling face, he felt the smoothness and warmth of the child's tiny body against his fingertips. Good, good, good. . . . He too might have known this goodness—but only if his life had been completely different from what in fact, in senseless and disgusting fact, it was. So never take yes for an answer, even when, as now, yes is self-evident. He looked again with eyes deliberately attuned to another wave length of value, and saw the caricature of a Memling altarpiece. "Madonna with Child, Dog, Pavlov and Casual Acquaintance."

Pala's values stand sturdily, however, against Farnaby's ironic probing; and most of the time his ridicule looks cheap against them. The tendency in these scenes is for the values to remain undisturbed but for the ridicule to redound onto Farnaby's head, just as in ancient times it was believed that an unjust curse or an unjust satire would redound onto the head of him who uttered it. Ridicule, many writers of the eighteenth century thought, is a test of truth. Huxley applies the test, although in carefully controlled doses; by incorporating hostile attitudes into his utopia, and assimilating them, to some degree he disarms them. This homeopathic use of satire in the literature of utopia is effective.

Most literary utopias, as we know, are not mere objects of contemplation, ideal and remote; but no more are they detailed blueprints for action. They are heuristic devices, models of the kind of society the authors think viable. Writers are likely to present enough details about how their respective societies function in matters economic, political, educational, and the like, so as to give some air of verisimilitude to their creations; but each is likely to concentrate on different matters, and details are less important than principles, less important than style and feel and tone. *Walden Two* and *Island* come together in interesting ways in a few details; both insist, for example (like many utopias before them), on the relaxation of family ties. But Skinner is relatively thorough on the economic structure of Walden Two and casual about education, whereas Huxley is most cavalier about economics, serious and interesting on education. These matters aside, however, the big difference is in the feel of the two societies.

Skinner makes a good deal of the authoritarian character of Walden Two, whose members entertain no nonsense about democracy. This is the totally planned society, structured so that a self-perpetuating elite shapes to their specifications the inhabitants of the world they control. To be sure, some of the methods of conditioning described seem ludicrously incommensurate with the claims made for them. It is the claims (and Frazier's compulsive anti-humanism) rather more than the techniques of teaching children self-control, or the methods used to decide that married couples should have separate rooms, that have given *Walden Two* its reputation as the devil's handbook. But the work must be taken in its own terms, and perhaps the reputation is justified. The inquiring Burris finds that the arts flourish at Walden Two, that the people have the illusion of freedom, that they seem relaxed and content. To a good many readers they also seem a little like zombies. Unless, like D. H. Lawrence, we are willing to accept the price exacted by the Grand Inquisitor along with the gifts he offers, we are unlikely to find Walden Two a notably good place. No matter how much he loves his children, Frazier has a whiff of brimstone about him, and the ironic distance between him at his worst and his creator Skinner is finally illusory. In a recent essay Skinner writes enviously about the assurance of the technology that went into designing the atomic bomb: "When we can design small social interactions and, possibly, whole cultures with the confidence we bring to physical technology, the question of value will not be raised."[7] That has about it the genuine ring of the final solution.

Against the authoritarianism and singlemindedness of *Walden Two*, where everything turns in on the idea of behavioral engineering, *Island* presents a notably open and flexible society, a model in some respects like that envisioned for a utopian future by Claude Lévi-Strauss, in which appropriate elements of both "cold" and "hot" societies are integrated.[8] *Island's* eclecticism is precisely what makes it interesting, its synthesis of ideas and modes of thought from East and West: Tantrik Buddhism and electrical generators, the arcadian tradition and the technological. In certain ways *Island* has affinities with *News from Nowhere*, particularly in its concern with the enrichment of sensual experience. Palanese religion, for example, contains a strong aesthetic element, giving a tone to life on the island utterly foreign to Walden Two (or to the Boston of *Looking Backward*, with which *Walden Two* has affinities), but quite in harmony with the rhythms of life that Morris dreamed of in his green and pleasant (and irreligious) land.

7. "The Design of Cultures," in H. Hoagland and R. W. Burhoe, eds., *Evolution and Man's Progress* (New York: Columbia University Press, 1962), p. 135.

8. *The Scope of Anthropology*, trans. Sherry O. Paul and Robert A. Paul (London: Cape, 1967), pp. 46–50. Primitive societies are cold in respect to historical temperature; they are static, their structure crystalline, designed to endure. Hot societies derive their extraordinary culture-producing energies from differentiations between castes and classes, between exploiter and exploited.

The difficulty with the book is largely one of style. In *Island* Huxley abandons his normal critical relationship to society and tries to will a new orientation—this time to a society he has created, one which embodies processes and goals that he values. The morally admirable effort is artistically disastrous. Huxley has no command of the celebratory style. The passages in the book which feel genuinely written are those dealing with Farnaby's past—return trips to Huxley's familiar hells; but when he tries to articulate the peculiar virtues of Palanese life he staggers between bathos and the inflated rhetoric of those who, without great poetic gifts, try to communicate the ineffable. As with many utopias, one has to distinguish between social and literary importance: *Island* may well have the one; it certainly does not have the other.

Walden Two and Pala have in common one major goal: within the limitations of the human condition, the happiness of their people. One can forgive these societies and their authors a good deal simply because they dare countenance so wildly anachronistic an aim. Twentieth-century literature can no more stomach happiness as an end in life than it can accommodate a hero. Dostoevski's Underground Man became an anti-hero at the moment he armed himself with misery against the principle of positive reinforcement and spat upon happiness as the potential subverter of his freedom. Lionel Trilling has shown how well our literature has absorbed the lesson.[9] By now, however, the pleasures of misery must be nearly exhausted, and it is refreshing to have two books that speak for happiness in the teeth of prescriptive despair. Our pleasure is mitigated, admittedly, by the terms in which Skinner, at least, speaks. The flight from freedom

9. "The Fate of Pleasure," in *Beyond Culture* (New York: Viking Press, 1965), pp. 57–87.

is one of the major themes of our time; and one can understand the tremendous appeal that the Grand Inquisitor exerts. Walden Two offers some of the benefits of allegiance to his cause. There is no denying their attractiveness. If it were not so, the dilemma would have no power to move us. But whereas the Grand Inquisitor demands a great act of abnegation from those who would be of his party, Skinner offers us a lollipop. The bathos, deliberately sought, reflects back onto Skinner and measures the society he creates. Huxley (despite didactic mynah birds and an utterly intolerable Palanese version of the Oedipus story) respects the magnitude of the issues involved in the utopian enterprise. Pala's people suffer, and storm troopers take over at the end; but the Palanese have created a society in which it is not a profanation to be happy.

In 1935, John Dewey, Charles Beard, and Edward Weeks named Bellamy's *Looking Backward* as second only to *Das Kapital* in the influence it had exerted on the world in the preceding fifty years. Three years earlier, however, *Brave New World* had been published and *Looking Backward* was already dead. The social effect of *Brave New World* was enormous—perhaps greater than Huxley intended—as it satirized not only the dehumanizing tendencies already present in our culture, but the very possibility of constructing a humane alternative to the appalling future awaiting us. *Brave New World* effectively satirized utopia out of existence. Thirty years later Huxley wrote *Island*. His extraordinary achievement is to have made the old utopian goal—the centrally human goal—thinkable once more.

Index